sew fun

20 PROJECTS FOR THE whole family

Deborah Fish

INTERWEAVE.
interweave.com

EDITOR Leslie T. O'Neill
TECHNICAL EDITOR Jacqueline Maxman
ILLUSTRATOR Missy Shepler
PHOTOGRAPHERS Joe Hancock except where noted
PHOTO STYLIST Pamela Chavez
ASSOCIATE ART DIRECTOR Julia Boyles
COVER & INTERIOR DESIGNER Julia Boyles
LAYOUT DESIGNER Dean Olson
PRODUCTION DESIGNER Katherine Jackson

 Interweave
A division of F+W Media, Inc.
201 East Fourth Street
Loveland, CO 80537
interweave.com

Manufactured in China by RR Donnelley Shenzhen

Library of Congress Cataloging-in-Publication Data

Fisher, Deborah, 1970-
Sew Fun: 20 Projects for the Whole Family / Deborah Fisher.
pages cm
Includes index.
ISBN 978-1-59668-760-8 (pbk)
ISBN 978-1-62033-038-8 (PDF)
1. Sewing. 2. Handicraft for children. I. Title.
TT705.F475 2013
646.2—dc23
2012048058

10 9 8 7 6 5 4 3 2 1

To my mother for the *how* and my girls for the *why*.

Acknowledgements

A huge thank you and a lifetime supply of chocolate (the really good stuff) . . .

. . . to **Allison Korleski and everyone at Interweave** for their faith in me and for all of their hard work to realize this book.

. . . to my agent, **Andrea Somberg,** who pops up even before I know I need her.

. . . to my fearless editor, **Leslie O'Neill,** for making me sound better than I am, and for her infinite patience with my ignorance.

. . . to my nifty husband, **Andrew,** whose insistent calm presence in the face of every one of my ridiculous ideas is simply astounding.

. . . to **my magical girls** who give their ideas, imaginations, and hugs with whole hearts.

. . . to the **countless friends and family** who gave freely of their love, support, sound advice, cheerleading, child care, and studio help from the initial sweet seed to the exhausting end. Yes, I mean you.

. . . to the **creative kids** I called upon to help in the uninhibited way only kids can (the Community Quilt makers: Dasi and Hazel Cash, Addy Docherty, Corby and Isabel Doerge, Ellie Ehrlich, Rachael Ehrlich, Kenny and Ryan Grigoletto, Isaac and Shoshana Lebo, Jack and Sam Loud, Lila and Manion Pessier, Justin and Sage Prinstein, Winnie Stach, and Henry Waugh; and the Indoor Snowman feature designers: Dasi and Hazel Cash, Renee Orlando, Joseph, Liana, and Michaela Prinzevalli).

. . . to **Eileen and Adam Fisher** for the hurricane-proof roots.

. . . to everyone at the **Bright Hopes Collaborative Quilt Project** for joining me on the journey.

. . . to **Susan Borger,** who is always there to show me the way when I ring the bell to summon the fiber fairy.

. . . to **Mordy and Oliver** for their sweet company—any extraneous cat hair is entirely their fault.

. . . to **Ann Loud** for her healing soul, huge heart, and amazing energy.

. . . and lastly, to the incredible, outrageous **Kelly Doerge,** whose generosity of talent, time, laughter, and spirit has been simply breathtaking. I couldn't have done it without you—you made it easy. Thanks, dude.

My cup runneth over. Thank you all.

Contents

in pursuit of
happy hands

I am a maker. An artist, designer, craftsperson, seamstress, sewist, whatever. Call me what you wish—I love to make things.

Years ago when I was an artist in residence in the Arts/Industry program at the Kohler Co. in Wisconsin, a world-renowned blacksmith asked me if I had kids. When I said no, he sighed and said, "The best thing you'll ever make."

He was right, of course. And when my first daughter was born, I wrote and told him so. Having kids didn't make me give up on making things, it just made it more fun. And now I get to share my love of making with my girls, just like my mother (and father!) did with me. The older my girls get, the more fun it is and the more I can see the maker in both of them.

Sew Fun: 20 Projects for the Whole Family evolved from my experience of finding a balance between guarding my own time and sharing what I love with my girls by making wonderful things with (and for) them. The bonus: I enjoy my time with them more if we are doing something I like to do.

The projects in *Sew Fun* can be made by yourself or with your kids. If you are making a gift (and you want it to be perfect) or just need some alone time, go to it. All of us makers need our own creative time. Mine sustains me. Simply, it feeds the soul. Ditch the guilt and get on with it.

But maybe you have a young friend with whom you want to share your love of making or whom you just can't keep out of your creative space. Even though all of these projects are great to make on your own, they each have ways to collaborate with your kids. Every set of instructions has a Kid Work box with recommendations on how your kids can make something with you. There are lots of great tips for working with kids in the Little Hands, Big Smiles section, too.

Some projects, like the There's No Place Like Home Pillows (page 134) and Fun Friends from Odds and Ends (page 106) incorporate your child's drawings. Others, like the Reading Time Quilt (page 140) and the Twice

the Smiles Quilt (page 146), are designed for you to make together and introduce your child to the fun of sewing wonderful things.

If you don't have a kid, borrow one. I guarantee his or her parents will thank you for introducing their child to a new creative world.

This is not all about fun. This is education in disguise. Learning incognito. Kids can learn color theory through fabric sorting, and they can enhance their fine motor skills by cutting and sewing. Math and patterning are all over the place in sewing, from using a ruler to figuring fractions and geometry. The finished projects in this book encourage dramatic and imaginative play as well as reading and storytelling. Also, you can encourage generosity and compassion by making and giving the Community Quilt (page 92) and the Twice the Smiles Quilt (page 146).

I designed these projects not just because my kids like them, but because I think they are fun, too. You won't want to relegate the finished products to your kid's room. You will want to see them in the rest of your home as well. You just might find yourself in make-believe lands, at spontaneous celebrations, and in improvised theatrical productions! Because kids create with such freedom and joy, you will learn as much from them as they learn from you.

Make no mistake. This book is not for kids. It is for you. But with these projects you get to make stuff while making kids happy. Smiles all around.

little hands, big smiles

How to Have Fun Sewing with Children

You can get kids involved in the actual making in small or large ways. How you do this will depend on the project you choose, the age of the child, and your personalities. Maybe you'll choose fabrics together, focusing on your son's favorite colors. You could supervise your daughter's first go at your sewing machine. You may even lead a bunch of cousins in a group project to present as a grandparents' gift.

From selecting fabrics to designing patterns to sewing the project, each project has a Kid Work list. I don't recommend ages for these jobs because even within a certain age group, fine motor skills and abilities vary widely. You will decide what makes sense for you and the kids you're sewing with.

How can you make this a wonderful experience for everyone?

Working Together

First, know yourself. I have trouble letting go of control when it comes to my projects. Not pretty, but I admit it.

When my older daughter was three and a half years old, she wanted to help me choose fabric for a doll. I cringed. I stressed. She pulled browns, oranges, reds, and purples from the scrap bag. I accepted that the doll would be a reject. Turns out, it was a great combination, and it is still one of my favorite dolls.

With the right balance, you can have as much fun as your little partner. You may be pleasantly surprised at the results, and you might even learn a thing or two from your own kid. If you like to be in control like I do, give yourself a good talking to before you start. (I need to do it every time I work with my girls.) Remind

yourself that this is not your personal project. You can say it belongs to both of you, but really it belongs to your child. You are there to provide technical support and to enjoy some special time together.

Also, know your kids. Do they like animals? Get them involved in choosing animal fabrics for the Reading Time Quilt (page 140). Do they lose interest when a project takes too long? Encourage them to help for just part of the project. Find their level of comfort and adjust as needed. Remember that this is supposed to be fun for both of you, and no one will have fun if the kids are frustrated.

Enjoy their freedom and creative abandon. You may find it catching.

Children are like wild animals: they can smell fear. Jump in with an open mind and a calm heart.

It's important to recognize when it isn't working and try another way. If working together on the same thing at the same time just isn't happening, try one of the projects that incorporate your children's drawings. For example, they do the drawing and you do the sewing with the There's No Place Like Home Pillows (page 134). Another great project for parallel making is the Indoor Snowman (page 62). You make the snowman, they make the features, and the actual objects don't meet up until the end. By working side by side but on your own parts, you can still have a great time together—and avoid some of the stress.

Let your kids help choose the fabric and trims. The more input they have in the decisions, the more excited they will be and the more they will love the final product. This may require some tongue biting and restraint on your part. You may hate orange. Get over it. On the other hand, when you get to choose materials, don't dumb down the colors. Out with insipid pastels for babies and pink for girls and blue for boys! Not only will it make your project unique, but you will be happy to have it in your home.

If you decide to make a project all by yourself, consider if your children would like a surprise or would like to watch as the project takes shape. Surprises are fun, but, depending on their ages, kids may not fully understand how the final object evolved. Showing them your progress here and there along the way can be exciting. It teaches them the process and shows them how much time and love you put into it.

The Question of Cutting

You'll notice that in all the Kid Work boxes in this book, cutting is rarely mentioned. Even though I have worked with children ages eight to eighteen to cut fabric for their own quilts, I prefer to focus on designing, sewing, and selecting materials when starting to sew with kids. These are the more immediate and visible parts of the process, so they will be the most joyful. Because cutting needs to be as precise as possible to make the rest of the project run smoothly, there is more room for frustration. Also consider your child's hand-eye coordination. The ability to use (very sharp) scissors or a rotary cutter may not be developed yet. Plus, there is the basic problem of body size when it comes to getting the proper leverage for rotary cutting.

But if you feel that your child is ready for cutting with scissors or a rotary cutter, by all means allow it. Remember, though, that safety and supervision are essential. You may want to purchase a cut-resistant glove made for rotary cutting that is worn on the non-dominant hand.

Sewing with Kids

I am often asked how to start a child off sewing. Many people believe handsewing is the simplest way to start. However, as much as I love handsewing, it can be the most frustrating. Often children's dexterity has not yet caught up with their desire to sew. Knots, tangles, too-large stitches, and general lumpiness in their projects can be disappointing—and cause them to give up altogether.

Surprising as it may be, I actually prefer teaching kids to sew with the machine first. Machine sewing is instant gratification, doesn't require the fine motor skills that handsewing does, and is a technique you can do together. Besides, you will be amazed at how fascinated kids are with the machine itself.

A more successful way to start handsewing with your child is a freestyle decorative embroidery project. Choose a small 7" (18 cm) good-quality embroidery hoop, a solid-color cotton fabric, and contrasting embroidery floss or pearl cotton. Start your child with a simple running stitch, then just let her go. She will be able to get used to the motion of sewing without the pressure of following a particular line or shape. The sewing will be decorative rather than functional, so it won't hold anything together or be part of a structure. After your child is more comfortable, have her draw a simple shape or design on the fabric and sew along the lines. You can then introduce machine sewing by helping her make her embroidery into a pillow or simple bag. Begin with the Simple Start Embroidery Project on page 14.

Introducing the Sewing Machine

Depending on the age of your children, they can actually help sew most of the projects in this book with your sewing machine. A great way to get your kids started is to let them work just the foot pedal. This allows them to be part of the action and get a feel for the machine, but it keeps their small fingers away from the needle. And it keeps you in the driver's seat.

Projects for Sewing Space Interlopers

Yikes! Here they come! Sometimes, those kids will find their way into your sewing space when it's inconvenient. Maybe you are working on a project that is not appropriate for them to help with, or maybe they just want to be near you but are not in the mood to help. While much depends on the age of your children, here are a few ideas for activities to keep everyone happy.

Scrap Designs on Flannel

If you have your own flannel design wall, make sure it reaches far enough to the floor so that little ones can reach it. You get the top and they get the bottom. Or put up a section of flannel especially for them. Set a box of scraps on the floor nearby and they are good to go. If they see you laying out a quilt, they may mimic what you are doing but will soon go on to their own free-form designs. Throw a few non-straight-sided shapes into the box to expand their selection.

Empty Spool and Ribbon Play

Save all those empty thread spools! Kids can thread the spools on ribbons or stack them like blocks. Have them tie one spool (and a feather or a bell!) on the end of a ribbon to make a cat toy.

Sorting Fun

If your interloper wants to help but the time is inconvenient for you, have bags or boxes full of scraps ready. Set them to sorting your fabric and scraps by color. Surprisingly helpful, this project makes them feel very important and is a great way to reinforce color identification.

Colored Pencil and Graph-Paper Drawings

Although you probably have plain paper available, there is something about graph paper that makes things very grown-up and official. Because I often use graph paper when planning quilts, my kids love to do the same. A pad of graph paper and an assortment of good colored pencils will make drawing time special. There are even free graph paper downloads online. Put in the size of the grid you want and change the shape from squares to circles to triangles to design your own paper and print out as many pages as you like. For children with good safety sense, add an electric pencil sharpener to the colored pencils, and they will be busy sharpening your pencils for hours. Of course you may not have any colored pencils left!

Sequin and Glue Pictures

You will, of course, already have sequins on hand to stitch special touches on Hazel Doll (page 112) or Laugh at Yourself Slippers (page 32). Sequins have an amazing ability to add magic to every situation without the mess of glitter. Add some paper and glue and your kids will wonder what special occasion prompted this project. And remember, glue is not just for sticking; it is a material in its own right! Concentrate on your own project and stop worrying about the glue puddles.

Little People

Have a supply of wooden doll pins or no-roll flat clothespins on hand. Kids can draw faces with markers or colored pencils. Supply glue, yarn, and fabric scraps for hair and clothes, as well as buttons, sequins, and other trims. These little dolls are so fun to make you may want to join in. This is a great project for many ages and mixed-age groups. It's also wonderful at a party.

Be sure to consider your children's ages and abilities as well as their interests and sensibilities when planning projects for your little interlopers. Design your own projects with stuff you have around. These projects are great distractions for kids while you work, but beware: you may find yourself joining them to make a sequin picture or two. You know you want to!

If you are lucky enough to have a speed control on your machine, fabulous. This is a switch, knob, or dial that lets you control the speed of the machine no matter how hard your kid steps on the pedal. I have this switch on my machine, and my daughter started sewing with me when she was two and a half years old. I put the switch on the lowest setting, and she stood on the pedal. I wouldn't have tried that with her if I didn't have the speed control, as I like my fingers the way they are, thank you very much.

If you don't have a speed control, you may want to wait until your child is a bit older and can understand the words "please slow down!" After all, sewing is not a race. Teenagers especially sometimes need reminding.

Alternatively, you can retrofit your pedal to only go one speed. Take a small block of wood and tape it securely to the side of your foot pedal, leaving a bit of space between the block and the bottom edge of the upper part of the pedal. How big a block of wood and exactly where you position it will depend on what type of pedal you have; experiment with it. The more space between the edge of the pedal and the wood, the faster your needle will go. Try a few seams out yourself to make sure that you are comfortable with the speed and that the block is securely attached. Of course, this method is not as adjustable as a built-in control, but it will give little kids a chance to try the machine (and save your hands).

If you think they are ready to use the sewing machine on their own, start with a nonessential project. Scraps are great for practice but are really boring. Kids are bound to lose interest. On the flip side, a complicated curved seam is probably not the way to start, either. Begin with

a simple quilt block, such as for the Twice the Smiles Quilt (page 146), or a basic bag, such as the Sew Sweet Strawberry Bag (page 36). Even the very forgiving Instant Drama Chenille Boa (page 40) is a fun first project! It may not be perfect, but it is all theirs, and they will have tremendous pride in it.

Continue to use the speed control on low or the retrofitted foot pedal. Sit on your child's left side so you can help guide the fabric if needed. Adding a piece of not-too-sticky blue painter's tape as a ¼" (6 mm) seam allowance guide all the way down the sewing bed is a great help in achieving even seams. A ¼" (6 mm) foot for your machine is also helpful.

I like to explain sewing this way. "Using a sewing machine is like riding a bike. If you pedal, the bike will go, but if you don't steer, you will end up in a ditch." Advise your kids not to look at the sewing machine needle because it will sew as long as you are stepping on the pedal. Encourage them to focus on matching the edge of the fabric to the edge of the blue tape—a nice and easy ride straight down the side of the road.

Most importantly, let go. I have taught many kids of varying abilities to make their own quilts. Barely a perfect ¼" (6 mm) seam on any of them. Who cares? Really. If you have to rip out a few spots because they wandered too far off course, have them sew another part of the project while you do that. They will get discouraged very quickly if they don't see forward movement on their project and if criticism takes over the fun. The quilt may not be as flat as you would like, but with your encouragement and support, they will be thrilled with their accomplishment. Yeah, smiles!

Choosing a Sewing Machine for a Child

Never buy a machine advertised as a children's sewing machine. There, I said it. Often they are not well made, they are battery operated, and they may even use a one-thread chain stitch that easily unravels rather than an actual two-thread machine stitch with a bobbin. Cheap plastic machines are not sew-worthy and will just cause frustration rather than create joy. If your children are going to do real sewing, then they need to use a real sewing machine. You need a basic model from a good brand, such as Pfaff, Janome, or Brother. If you can swing it, a Bernina is wonderful.

A straight stitch, a zigzag stitch, and the ability to swap in a walking foot are all you need. My feeling is that all those fancy decorative machine embroidery stitches programmed into your machine only thwart creativity. You need just one sewing machine for two of you to work together.

Ready, Set, Draw

Many projects in this book incorporate your children's drawings, paintings, and creative ideas. I can't tell you how thrilled they will be when they see their pictures translated into fabric and thread. Think outside the patterns and instructions and go for it!

When you need one of their drawings for a project, don't tell them what you want. Just have a great big drawing and painting session. Suggest the topics you're looking for, such as a dream house or a self-portrait, but don't be pushy or critical. It sucks the fun out of it for everyone.

My girls and I sewed up House Pillows (page 134) inspired by their drawings of imaginary houses.

Better yet, start collecting drawings before you need them. As wonderful drawings and paintings come home from school or are made at home, keep a file. You may even want to categorize it by subject matter (people, animals, buildings, etc.). You will be all set when you are ready to stitch up a new Fun Friend (page 106) or There's No Place Like Home Pillow (page 134).

Also, have extra drawings to choose from. Lots. Tons. What looks wonderful on the page does not always translate well into sewn three-dimensional items. With some practice, you will be able to recognize what is likely to work and what

won't, but be prepared for some trial and error. I have a pile of unused doll faces that were adorable when they were drawn but were downright frightening when embroidered.

Different drawings may work better for different projects. For example, the Topsy-Turvy Story Quilt (page 56) works best with simple shapes, while a little line drawing is the way to go for an embroidery on Hazel Doll's coat (page 120).

Give yourself some creative license. You may need to simplify a drawing, separate out various elements, or combine others to make it work technically or fit within the confines of a particular project. Copy the drawing so you can keep the original intact and then cut and paste it as necessary.

Safety Always

As always, safety. Boring, I know, but essential. Nothing sucks the fun out of sewing like blood on the fabric and a trip to the emergency room. Rotary cutters, pins, needles, scissors, irons, and sewing machines can be very hazardous. Always be vigilant and aware, especially when working with younger children. With care, children can actually use a variety of sewing equipment without incident.

The safety first rule also extends to the materials you use, especially if you're creating gifts for younger children. Double-stitching seams and using a shorter stitch length will make seams stronger and less likely to tear. Avoid buttons and other detachable items in favor of embroidery. Even when making projects for older children, beware of younger children in the house who have access to the same toys.

For some projects, like the Instant Drama Chenille Boa (page 40) or Insect Capes (page 28), supervision extends past the making to the playing. Never let children play unattended with anything that goes around their necks.

Go Sew

Recently my daughter asked me to teach her how to crochet. I told her I didn't know how, but that we could figure it out together. Making things is a process. You don't have to know everything—what's the adventure in that? Plan on learning together. Be bold. Draw, cut, sew, and take an ice cream break. Find yourself a kid and get busy making wonderful things!

Photos by Joe Coca

Simple Start Embroidery Project

This is a great project to start your kids off sewing. They learn to hand-sew with simple embroidery stitches, which don't have to be structurally sound. You can also introduce them to machine sewing by helping them make the embroidery project into a basic bag or a simple pillow. Or mount it on wood to highlight the stitching as a work of art. Kids can gain confidence for bigger projects when they start off learning basic skills.

MATERIALS

* ⅓ yd (30.5 cm) of solid-color cotton quilting-weight fabric

* Contrasting embroidery floss

TOOLS

* Basic Sewing Kit

* 7" (18 cm) embroidery hoop

* Fabric markers (optional)

FINISHED SIZE

The finished embroidery sample is 12" × 12" (30.5 × 30.5 cm).

– – – – – – – – – – – – – – – –

You may want to have several pieces of fabric cut and ready to go in case your kids' first attempts at embroidery turn into crazy tangles and they want to start again. Don't waste time taking out all the floss. Just pop one piece of fabric out of the hoop and pop in a new one. You can even announce at the beginning that the first try is simply practice.

① Cut a 12" (30.5 cm) square of fabric and slip it into the embroidery hoop. Use two strands of floss so you can double the thread and knot the ends together, creating four strands.

One of the difficult parts of hand-sewing for children is learning to avoid pulling the needle off the thread. Doubling the thread or floss and knotting the ends together will solve that frustration.

② Starting with the knot on the back side, show them how to make a basic running stitch. Prepare a few needles threaded with different colors of floss.

If your kids are like mine, their initial mistakes will be making very large stitches and wrapping the floss around the hoop. Don't worry so much about a few huge stitches. You can always tack them down later to keep them from getting caught. Encourage making small stitches, but mostly encourage having fun. Have them try straight lines, wavy lines, any-which-way lines **(FIGURE 1)**.

③ When you think your kids are ready to move on, try transferring a simple shape onto the fabric for them to follow. Or, they could draw on the fabric with fabric markers and then choose a line to embroider over to add texture, such as a flower stem, a dress outline, or a smile. As they become more comfortable, introduce other stitches like the backstitch (see page 20 for my go-to stitch!).

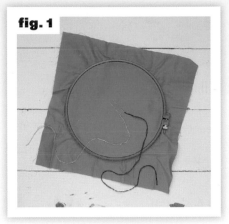

fig. 1

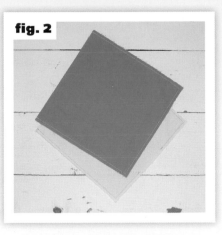

fig. 2

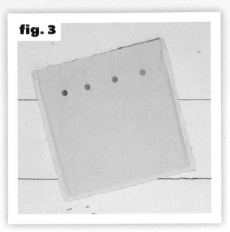

fig. 3

When you have lovely embroidery and proud children, work with them to transform their projects into a bag, a pillow, or a wall hanging.

A Basic Bag

To make the embroidery into a bag that they can carry with them and show off their work, you'll also need ⅓ yd (30.5 cm) of cotton fabric for the lining and ¾ yd (68.5 cm) of a ½" (1.3 cm) ribbon to make the handle.

① Trim the embroidery to 9" × 9" (23 × 23 cm). Cut one more 9" × 9" (23 × 23 cm) piece of the same fabric for the back of the bag. Cut two 9" × 9" (23 × 23 cm) pieces of the lining fabric for the bag lining.

② If there are lots of loose threads or some big stitches on the back of the embroidery, you should make a lining for the bag so the threads don't get caught. Match the two lining pieces right side together. Sew down one side, turn the corner, pivoting the fabric 90 degrees with the needle still in the fabric, and then sew 3" (7.5 cm) on the next side. Leave 2½" (6.5 cm) open for turning, and then continue sewing 3" (7.5 cm) down the rest of the side. Turn the corner and sew up the third side.

③ To make the outside of the bag, match the embroidery with the backing, right sides together. Sew three sides, making sure the embroidery is oriented correctly to the bottom. Clip the two sewn corners and turn the bag right sides out **(FIGURE 2)**.

④ To add a handle, make a mark 2½" (6.5 cm) from each side seam along the open edge. Cut two 11" (28 cm) pieces of ribbon. Pin an end of the ribbon to each mark, matching the ribbon's raw ends to the fabric's raw edges. Turn the bag over and do the same on the other side. Baste the ribbon handles onto the bag.

⑤ Place the bag inside the bag lining so the right sides are together and the open edges match **(FIGURE 3)**. Sew around the top edge to connect the outside and the lining. Turn the bag right side out through the opening in the lining, then stitch it closed. Push the lining into the bag. Press. Topstitch ½" (1.3 cm) from the edge around the bag opening.

A Simple Pillow

Make a sweet little pillow and give it a spot front and center on your family room couch.

① Trim the embroidery to 9" × 9" (23 × 23 cm). Cut a 9" × 9" (23 × 23 cm) piece of fabric for the back.

② Pin the squares with right sides together. Sew around the outside of the pillow, leaving an opening of about 4" (10 cm) in the middle of one side. Clip the corners and turn right side out.

③ Press the pillow and stuff to desired fullness. Handsew the opening closed. Use an invisible ladder stitch or, for a fun detail, whipstitch the opening closed with contrasting or coordinating floss. You can even make a uniform whipstitch (See Tools and Techniques, page 16) around the entire edge as special trim.

A Work of Art

Show your kids that their sewing is just as valuable as their paintings and drawings by creating artwork for your walls.

① Use purchased wooden stretchers or a block of wood to stretch their artwork for hanging. If you are using a block of wood, drill a hole near the top for hanging.

② Place the embroidery right side down on a clean table. Set the frame or wood block down in the center of the fabric. Work your way back and forth around the fabric, stapling first one side and then the opposite side to the back of the frame or block. Finish it by neatly tucking in the corners.

tools and techniques

So here's the deal: I am not a technical sewer. I break the "rules" all the time, but mostly I just make up my own rules. What's the worst that can happen? Things are a bit crooked or you have to tear out a seam or two. The kids in your life will think you and the project are fabulous anyway. Lose the fear. There are lots of things in life to be afraid of, but sewing is not one of them. If you are worried about cutting into your favorite material or are uneasy about forging ahead, make samples out of muslin first. It will build your confidence and give you a great reference library.

Still, my just-go-ahead-and-do-it attitude toward technique does not equal poor craftsmanship. Fine craftsmanship is something every maker should always aspire to. Of course, working with children does not always make this easy. Try to have different standards for yourself and for them. As they get more experience, the craftsmanship gap will close.

This book assumes that you have basic sewing knowledge, but some techniques that I use in these projects may be new to you. Use them as a guide and do what works best for you. Experiment, curse, smile, do a happy dance. Or as we like to say in my studio (with much love, of course, and when no children are in earshot), "Just shut up and sew."

I am also not much for lots of specialty tools. I prefer a solid collection of basics, like those in my Basic Sewing Kit. For each project in this book, you will need your own Basic Sewing Kit. Some of the more advanced projects require additional tools to complete. Your tool preferences are as individual as your ways of working, and I encourage you to discover what works best for you as well as for your child.

The Basic Sewing Kit

These tools are all you need for most of the projects in this book and those you tackle beyond *Sew Fun:*

✳ A sewing machine

✳ A rotary cutting set that includes a self-healing mat, a rotary cutter with extra blades, and a gridded ruler

✳ One pair of large 8" (20.5 cm) scissors and one pair of small 3" (7.5 cm) embroidery scissors

✳ Paper scissors

✳ A seam ripper

✳ Extra sewing-machine needles

✳ An assortment of handsewing and embroidery needles

✳ Pins

✳ Iron and ironing board

✳ Tape measure

✳ Pencil and other marking tools

✳ Ballpoint bodkin, tube turner, and other turning tools

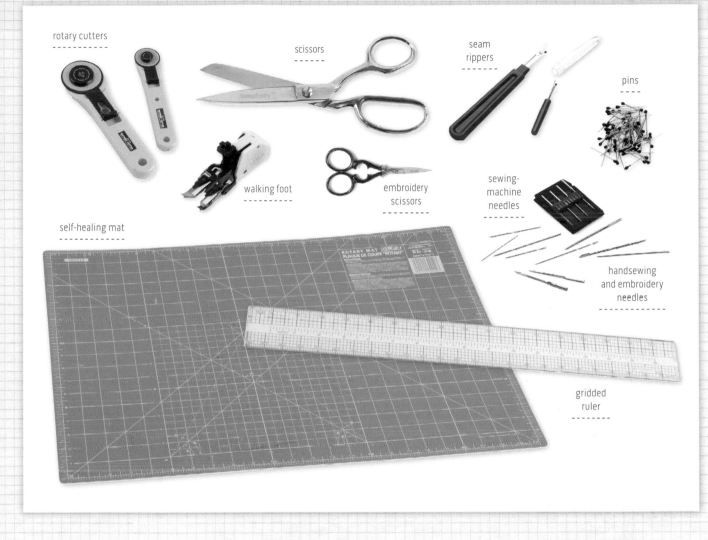

rotary cutters

scissors

seam rippers

pins

walking foot

embroidery scissors

sewing-machine needles

self-healing mat

handsewing and embroidery needles

gridded ruler

Sewing Machine and Feet

Don't let those fancy does-everything-but-the-laundry sewing machines intimidate you. All you need is a good-quality machine that makes a straight stitch and a zigzag. Still, a few different feet for your machine can elevate your sewing. I change the feet on my machine often. These are the ones I like to keep handy:

* A ¼" (6 mm) piecing foot, which makes it easier to keep seam allowances even

* A walking foot for quilting and for sewing two different types of fabric together

* A zipper foot for sewing close to trims, boning, or heavy interfacing

* A darning or free-motion foot for free-motion quilting and machine embroidery

* An edgestitch foot, also called a topstitch or blind-hem foot, for sewing close to an edge or seam

I especially like my edgestitch foot. Different brands may call this foot by different names, but usually it has a center guide. I use it to guide along a topstitching edge or keep a zigzag stitch on center when butt joining (page 19). Pop in this foot and forever end the frustration of wobbling around and cursing.

tools and techniques

Rotary Cutting Equipment

Get a mat as big as you can find, afford, and have the space for. For gridded rulers, start with one that's 8½" × 12" (21.5 × 30.5 cm) or 6" × 12" (15 × 30.5 cm). I also like an 8½" × 24" (21.5 × 61 cm) or 6" × 24" (15 × 61 cm) ruler and a 15" (38 cm) square. As you make more projects you will learn what size rulers work for you, but a few basic sizes will help you get started. A 48 mm cutter and blade is fine, but you may also want to try the 60 mm cutter for large projects and cutting multiple layers at once or the 28 mm for cutting curves.

Scissors

When I was little, my mother sent away a coupon from the back of a Cheerios box to get a set of orange-handled Fiskars scissors for me, one pair of 8" (20.5 cm) sewing scissors, and a smaller pair of embroidery scissors. Even though I have added to my collection, I still use those scissors every day. Get yourself some good scissors.

Also useful are a pair of small curved embroidery scissors, a pair of sharp snips, and a pair just for paper. Make sure you also have scissors that are appropriately sized for the hands of the child working with you.

Colored Pencils and Marking Tools

When tracing patterns onto fabric I like to use soft colored pencils, as long as the marks won't show. Colored pencil will not come off your fabric! They are also great for sketches and designs. Have a good sharpener handy.

For temporary marking, such as for embroidery designs, I use wax-free transfer paper made for sewing projects. A package of white, blue, and yellow will take you through most colors of background fabric.

Tube Turner and Bodkin

You may wonder what you did without these few little inexpensive extras to throw into your sewing kit.

A tube turner with several different-diameter plastic tubes and wooden sticks works great for turning doll and animal legs and other tubes. The plastic tube goes into the right side of a fabric tube, and you use the stick to push the fabric into the plastic tube, turning it right side out.

A ballpoint bodkin looks like a very large needle with a big eye and a ball instead of a point. Use the bodkin to thread ribbon and drawstrings through casings. Use the ballpoint to help smooth curves.

A Design Board

A design board is a wonderful thing for you and any kids you may have about—optional but fabulous. If you have an open wall, pin up a neutral flannel sheet. Get a sheet as big as your free wall so you have room for a big quilt, space to work on several projects at once, or room for you and your kids. If you have no walls to spare, get a piece of cardboard or foam core and cover it with flannel. Store your movable wall in a closet or under the bed when not in use. Keep a box of fabric and felt scraps nearby for whenever your kid is struck with inspiration.

Fabrics

This book contains projects with a variety of fabrics from cotton to felt, wool, linen, plush, satin, and even metallics and velvets. These materials can add richness to your projects and make them extra wonderful. Be sure to test these fabrics if you have not worked with them before. Pins and especially basting will keep ornery seams where they need to be, and a walking foot is a great help in evenly feeding two different or shifting fabrics.

Fill

You can use either cotton or polyester fill for the projects that require stuffing, such as the dolls in the Love chapter (page 104), the Over in the Meadow Landscape Rug movable elements (page 68), and the There's No Place Like Home Pillows (page 134). Polyester fill is the most common and stable fill, but I prefer cotton. Cotton fill will give your project more substance and weight, a quality I like. It can be a bit lumpy to deal with but is also more moldable so you can get it just where you need it. Cotton fill can clump when machine washed so I tend to use it more for projects that will be surface cleaned.

Techniques to Sew By

These projects are made with a variety of fun techniques and degrees of complexity, including a few that you may not have yet encountered. They can expand your making repertoire exponentially and help you to complete each project with extra joy as well as excellent craftsmanship. All the projects in this book use a ¼" (6 mm) seam allowance unless otherwise noted.

Using a Child's Drawings

Many projects in this book incorporate your child's drawings, which you will need to copy and probably resize to use. You can either take the drawing to your local copy center and have it enlarged on one piece of paper in the size you want or copy it yourself on the smaller paper used in your home printer/copier. You may need to enlarge the drawing in sections, moving the original around to get all parts enlarged and then taping all the pieces together, matching the lines.

Now that you have the drawing at the correct size for your project, you will need to transfer it to fabric. My preferred method is to use wax-free transfer paper in a color that contrasts with my fabric. Place the transfer paper colored side down on your fabric. Position the copy of the drawing on top and use a blunt point, such as a knitting needle, to trace the drawing onto the fabric. The transfer lines brush off easily without washing. If you find the lines brushing off as you sew, you can just retransfer some of the lines.

Working with Ribbon

When the ends of the ribbon will not be sewn into a seam, you should treat them so they don't fray. Natural fibers are wonderful to use, but the ends must be sewn in or hemmed to avoid fraying. With synthetic fibers, you can melt the ends to seal them. Tie back your hair and have a container of water nearby just in case. Light a match and hold it just close enough to the cut end to melt the first few threads. Run the match carefully down the end until it is sealed. You may need to go through several

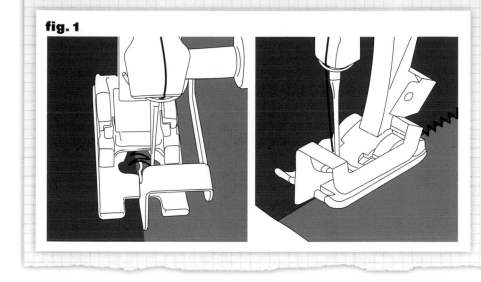

fig. 1

matches as you get comfortable with this. You can also use a lighter or a candle, but look out for dripping wax.

Felting Wool Fabrics

Felted wool fabrics are wool knits or wovens that have been shrunk and felted—yes, just like that special sweater that ended up in the wash! Check out your local thrift store for old sweaters or blankets in a variety of colors and textures. Throw them in your washer and dryer and see what comes out. Repeat if you want more shrinkage. Not very scientific, but that is part of the fun! You can also experiment with wool yardage from the fabric store.

Sewing Butt Joins

Several projects in this book use thicker felted wool or felt that will not fray and is perfectly suited to **butt joining**. The two fabrics to be joined are butted up against each other and sewn with a zigzag stitch **(FIGURE 1)**. I like to use a wide zigzag with a medium length, but you should experiment to see what will work best with your fabrics.

Use an edgestitch foot if you have one. Position the center divider of the foot between the two fabrics to be joined. The stitches will go over the foot and slide off the back of the divider. This keeps your join in the center of the zigzag. Gently guide the two pieces toward the center as you sew. Steam and press to ease any wrinkles back in place.

Sewing Curves

With a little practice, sewing curves on your machine can be a piece of cake. I like to use a ¼" (6 mm) piecing foot to help make my seams more precise. If your machine has a button that will automatically put the needle down when you stop, activate it. If not, do that by hand. Keep your right hand on the presser foot lift. Take it off if you need to put the needle down by turning your wheel or pressing a button, depending on your machine. Keep your left hand on the fabric. Take a few stitches and then put the needle down. Pull the presser foot up slightly. Pivot and then put the presser foot down.

Take your time and don't try to take too many stitches at once. On tight or very important curves you may be making only one or two stitches before you pivot. A little practice will make your hand motions as well as your curve smooth.

For all of your lovely sewing to shine, you need to clip and press the seams carefully. Clipping is taking small snips in the seam allowance along curves so the fabric will lie smoothly inside the seam. Make sure you do not clip any stitches. Smooth the seams from the inside in addition to the outside and gently use a pin to tuck in any little points sticking up.

Sewing by Hand

Even those of us who use the sewing machine for everything need to pick up a needle now and then for non-decorative sewing. Take your time when handsewing and your project will go from "meh" to "wow!"

The invisible **ladder stitch (FIGURE 2)** is a must for beautiful projects. Whether you are closing an opening on a doll or pillow or handsewing a binding on a quilt, this is the one to master for professional looking projects.

If you are sewing two folded edges together, insert the needle inside one of the folded sides and come out right on the fold. Go straight across the opening and to the opposite fold and insert the needle right in the fold. Slide the point of the needle inside the fold for about ⅛" (3 mm). I call this *riding the fold*. Come out right on the fold. Go straight across the opening to the opposite fold and insert the needle right in the fold. Ride the fold for ⅛" (3 mm) and come out right on the fold. Continue going straight back and forth along the opening.

When sewing one folded edge and one flat side, such as attaching a quilt binding to a quilt, ride the needle on the underside of the fabric on the flat side instead of in the fold.

A **whipstitch (FIGURE 3)** is another way to close an opening; however, the thread will show. This is a much simpler stitch for a child. Hide the knot on the inside of a fold, then push the needle through on the outside of the project just below the fold. Wrap the thread across the two folds and insert the needle just below the fold on the opposite side. Come back out on the original side just below the fold and further along the opening than the original stitch. Repeat down the length of the opening, whipping the thread over the folds.

A **blanket stitch (FIGURE 4)** can be used to sew openings closed as well as for appliqué and as a decorative embroidery stitch. To sew an opening closed, insert the needle inside the fold on one side and come out of the fold. Make a loose stitch diagonally back and to the right of where you came out of the fold. From the back, bring the needle underneath the loose stitch. Gently adjust the thread so the first stitch is a right angle. The stitch should lie along the seam; turn the corner where the thread is holding it in place, and then go perpendicularly up to where it goes into the fabric. Continue taking stitches up to the right, coming around the back, and then looping through the stitch.

Embroidery Basics

When I embroider kid drawings and lettering, I like the original artwork to shine. So instead of fancy embroidery stitches, I stick to the basics. Although an embroidery hoop makes a project easier for children

to handle, I do not use one myself. Do what works best for you.

Mostly I use a **backstitch (FIGURE 5)**. Think of your stitching line as a dotted line. The dots are where the needle goes. The spaces in between are where the thread goes. Insert your needle from the back of the project to the front at the first dot and make one stitch to the back, and then one up to the front again (a running stitch). Insert the needle back one stitch to fill the empty space. Skip another two spaces and bring the needle up on the far side. Insert the needle back one stitch to fill that empty space. Repeat going two spaces forward on the back of the project and one space backward on the front of the project.

To fill in spaces with a **satin stitch (FIGURE 6)**, start from one side of a shape and make a stitch to the opposite side. Come back up right next to where you started the first stitch. Make a stitch across the shape and insert the needle right next to where you ended the first stitch. Continue stitching back and forth across the shape until it is filled in. If your shape is wider than an inch, make several back stitches across the width. If your stitches are too long, they will catch on things.

French knots (FIGURE 7) are great for little accents, flower centers, and eyes. Bring the needle up from the back to the front of the fabric. Wrap the thread or floss around the needle three times and, holding onto the wrapped floss, insert the needle back down through the original hole. Pull the needle through.

A **chain stitch (FIGURE 8)** makes a wider, decorative line. Bring the needle up from the back to the front of the fabric. Go back down into the

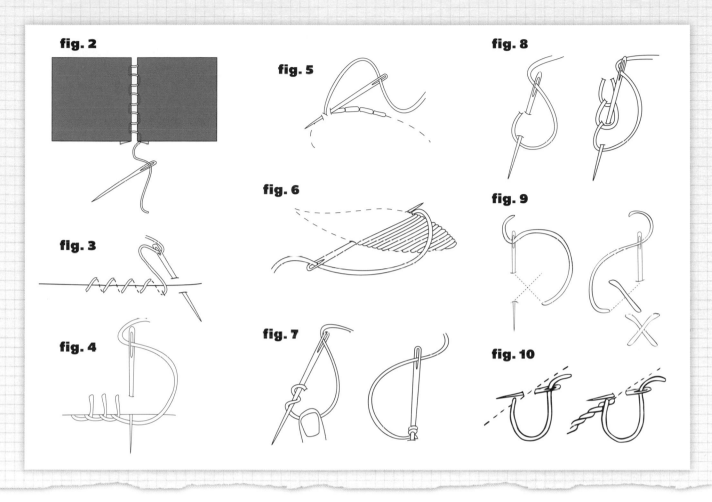

fig. 2

fig. 5

fig. 8

fig. 3

fig. 6

fig. 9

fig. 4

fig. 7

fig. 10

original hole, leaving a small loop on the top. Bring the needle up one stitch length away and through the loop. Pull the embroidery floss gently so the original loop is flush with the new stitch. Go back down in the hole for the second stitch and leave a loop. Each stitch secures the previous stitch as they are chained together.

A **cross-stitch (FIGURE 9)** is another decorative stitch. Consider these stitches as a series of Xs in a row. Bring the needle up through the bottom right corner of the X. Go back down at the top left corner. Come back up through the bottom left corner. Come back down through the top right corner. Repeat these steps so

that the Xs connect. For added detail, use a contrasting color to make a running stitch so the top of the stitch goes just over the center of the X.

Stem stitch (FIGURE 10) has a similar look to backstitch, but the stitches are at an angle and overlap each other. This creates a thicker line. Draw a line where you want your stitching to be. You will stitch on either side of the line, not directly on it. Insert your needle from the back of the fabric to the front, just above the line. Insert the needle just below the line, making one stitch along the line. Come back up above the line at the midway point of your first stitch. Continue stitching along the line in this way.

Appliqué

Appliqué is a wonderful technique for pictorial work. Choose from meditative hand work to fast straight-line machine appliqué or anything in between that fits your time restrictions and aesthetics. When designing appliqués with more than one section, think about how the pieces will be layered.

For **machine appliqué**, you do not need a seam allowance, so cut your pieces right to size. Pin the pieces to your background fabric. You can use a zigzag stitch, buttonhole stitch, or any other machine stitch to carefully sew around each piece. Even simpler is a straight stitch sewn about ⅛"

to ¼" (3 to 6 mm) in from the edge. Stitch around each piece once, twice, or even three times for a casual, sketchy look.

Hand appliqué is, of course, more time consuming, but a lovely addition as a detail or for an important project. Cut the pieces ⅛" (3 mm) larger than your shape all around. Pin the piece to the background. Using the point of the needle, turn under the ⅛" (3 mm). Use an invisible ladder stitch to sew all around the appliqué.

Quilting

After you have finished your beautiful quilt top, you need to put it together with the batting and the backing. Kids love to help with this, but make sure you have all the parts ready so they don't wander off while waiting for you to get organized.

Press the top. Cut the batting a few inches larger than your quilt top all the way around. For the quilts in this book, the backings are pieced horizontally. Cut the backing yardage in half widthwise. Trim the selvedges off one long side of each piece. Match those two trimmed edges right sides together and sew using a ½" (1.3 cm) seam allowance. Press the seam open to eliminate bulk when you are quilting.

Lay your backing right side down on the floor. Using masking tape or painter's tape, tape the backing to the floor, working back and forth on opposite sides so the fabric remains even all the way around. The backing should be taut but not tight. Lay the batting on top of the backing, smoothing it out from the center. Place the quilt top on top of the batting right side up and again smooth it out from the center, working toward

I used straight-line stitching and "valley stitching" on the Twice the Smiles Quilt (page 146) to emphasize its geometric shapes.

the edge. You can tape the top down if you wish.

Use regular or quilting safety pins to pin the three layers together. Start from the center and try to pin at least every 8" (20.5 cm) or so. Remember that the pins will be the only thing holding your quilt together until you quilt or tie it. Depending on the size of their hands and their dexterity, some kids have trouble with the safety pins. Try having them just put the pins in the quilt while you follow them to close the pins. Remove the tape and trim the backing even with the batting.

There are several options for completing your quilt. Both hand- and machine-quilting a larger quilt can seem daunting. Choose the technique that not only visually fits the quilt you are making, but that also makes sense for you.

Machine-quilting can be straight-line quilting, valley stitching, or free-motion quilting.

Straight-line stitching is just that: sewing straight lines throughout

the entire quilt. You can create an amazing variety of designs just with straight lines: stripes, zigzags, squares, and grids. Use a walking foot to keep the layers together. This technique is great for getting older kids started on quilting.

Valley stitching is also known as stitch in the ditch. I have taken it upon myself to rename it valley stitching because I, for one, would rather be in a valley than a ditch. This technique also uses straight lines and a walking foot, but the stitches are placed right in the seams of the pieced top. This requires good concentration but can be great for highlighting various blocks or patches on a quilt.

Free-motion quilting is basically drawing with stitches. Instead of the pencil moving over the paper, you are moving the quilt sandwich under the needle. Use a free-motion foot and lower the feed dogs on your machine.

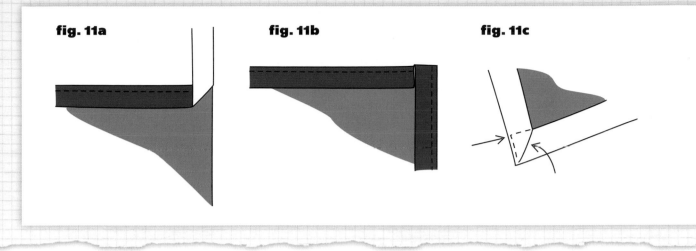

fig. 11a   **fig. 11b**   **fig. 11c**

Hand-quilting can be an art within itself, but it doesn't have to be so serious. While many quilters use a large hoop and thimble for hand-quilting, I employ my usual "no rules, few tools" method and simply use a quilting needle and thread. I think of hand-quilting as simply a small running stitch. Use a short quilting needle, called a between, and rock your needle up and down to make a few stitches on your needle and then pull the stitches through. The goal is to make your stitches small and even and the same on the back as the front. However, handwork is handmade, and good craftsmanship doesn't mean looking like a machine. The beauty is in seeing the hand.

Tying is the simplest and quickest way of joining your quilt sandwich together, and it's an effective way to get kids involved. Use embroidery floss, pearl cotton, or any other decorative, strong yarn. Leave the end of the floss unknotted. Take one stitch into the quilt sandwich and then back up again, leaving a few inches or several centimeters of the tail. Knot the two ends together and trim to about ½" (1.3 cm). Make sure you have enough of a stitch on the back to hold the layers together, but not so much to cause a pucker when

the knot is tied, about ³⁄₁₆" (5 mm). You can also start from the back of the quilt so the stitch is on the front of the quilt and the knot is on the back.

Now it is time to bind your quilt. My favorite way to bind a quilt is sleek and simple. Cut enough 2½" (6.5 cm) wide strips of fabric to generously go all the way around your quilt. Trim off any selvedge ends. Make one long binding by sewing the short ends of the strips right sides together. Some quilters like to piece the strips at an angle to eliminate bulk, but here my lazy side is showing—I don't think it's worth the trouble. Press the seams open. Fold the binding in half down the entire length with wrong sides together and press.

Starting in the center of the bottom side of the quilt, match the raw edge of the binding to the raw edge of the front of the quilt. Using a ½" (1.3 cm) seam allowance, sew the binding to the quilt, starting 2" (5 cm) from the beginning of the binding. You will need to adjust this seam measurement if you have cut the strips a different size than 2½" (6.5 cm). Experiment with a small section to make sure you have your seam allowance correct.

To make mitered corners, sew the binding to ½" (1.3 cm) from the next side. Fold the loose part of the binding to the side so the binding folds at a 45-degree angle in the corner **(FIGURE 11a)**. Then fold the binding back toward the next quilt edge, creating a straight fold at the previous edge and matching the raw edge of the binding with the quilt edge **(FIGURE 11b)**. Start sewing this side ½" (1.3 cm) in from the corner. Repeat the steps for sewing the sides and the corners until you are back where you started.

Stop sewing 2" (5 cm) from the beginning of the binding. Trim the binding to 4" (10 cm). Fold back the end of the binding 1" (2.5 cm) and overlap with the beginning of the binding. Continue sewing across the overlap until you are back where you started. If the small amount of bulk bothers you, you can piece the ends together. Fold the binding around to the back of the quilt to encase the raw edge **(FIGURE 11c)**.

Handsew the binding into place with a small whipstitch or invisible ladder stitch.

fig. 12　　fig. 13　　fig. 14

Fabric Cutting Techniques

No need to panic when a project requires cutting on the bias! Woven fabrics are actually a grid with warp threads going one way and weft threads going perpendicular to the warp. "Bias" means diagonal—a 45-degree angle to the straight warp and weft threads. Even though there are all kinds of fancy ways to cut on the bias, my approach aims to be simple and direct.

With the fabric flat in front of you, take the lower right corner and fold it up to the left so the bottom edge of the fabric is even with the left edge. Line up your gridded ruler so it is square with the folded edge and the original corner that you folded up. Cut from the fold to the corner. Use the cut edge on both of the pieces to cut parallel strips to the required width. If your gridded ruler is not long enough, use another ruler or straightedge to extend the line to the corner.

Sometimes you may want to cut an image out of a piece of fabric to make a special patch for a quilt or a doll. This is called **fussy cutting.**

Double-check your fabric before you start cutting to make sure you have enough of the required images. You may need to cut six animals from your animal fabric, but if the lion is right next to the hippo, you may have to sacrifice one to get the other. Remember to add a ¼" (6 mm) seam allowance when you are planning and cutting.

A Few Tricks up Your Sleeve

With a few fun extras, you can make sewing these projects a particularly special experience for you and your kids. These are great ways to incorporate the talents of all of your kids, from the youngest to the oldest!

How to Make Felt Balls

Why are felt balls so much fun to use? Pop one on the top of almost anything and you have instant whimsy. Make yourself a little stash of all different sizes and colors to have at the ready. They are also a great wet and soapy project to do with kids.

You can felt smaller balls by hand. Fluff up a bunch of wool roving, making sure the wool fibers are going in different directions. As the wool felts, it will shrink, so keep that in mind when deciding how much roving to use. Dip the fluffy roving into hot, soapy water. The water should be as hot as you can make it and still be safe. Roll the roving into a ball between your palms. Continue to dip and roll until the wool has become a lovely ball **(FIGURE 12)**.

To make larger balls, you need some old stockings or knee-highs and your washer and dryer. Fluff up a big pile of roving and stuff it into the toe of a stocking, then tie off the stocking **(FIGURE 13)**. You can add as many balls of roving as you have room for down the length of the stocking. Throw the stocking in the washer with some soap on a hot-water setting; you may need to repeat this step and several wash cycles to fully felt the balls. When the balls are almost as felted as you like, put the stocking in the dryer. The dryer will continue to tighten things up a bit **(FIGURE 14)**.

Cut the knots in your stocking. The fibers will have worked their way through the stocking so you will need to peel the stocking off the balls.

Recruit your children to make felt balls that they can use as play trees and shrubs for the Over in the Meadow Landscape Rug (page 68). Leftovers can easily be turned into a handy pincushion.

Making a Label for Your Quilt

Any quilt is made extra special with a handmade label. Make it any size you like, mix and match techniques, and get the kids involved.

To draw a label by hand, iron a matching size piece of freezer paper to fabric and use fabric markers. The paper will keep your fabric stable as you write and draw. Hand-appliqué the label to the back of your finished quilt.

You can also make a label on the computer using simple word processing or more advanced graphic programs. Print your label on sew-on, printable fabric. Be sure you get the kind that is appropriate for your printer.

For an extra special label, hand-embroider the recipient's name onto coordinating fabric.

Rickrack trim is especially nice on a round or oval label as a fun little frame. Trim the label to include a seam allowance that is half the width of the rickrack. Pin the rickrack around the edge of the label, matching one edge of the rickrack with the raw edge of the label and the other edge of the rickrack toward the center of the label. Sew the rickrack to the label down the center of the trim. Turn under the seam allowance and handsew the label to the quilt.

Even a simple name tag becomes extra special when you embroider it by hand and stitch it to the back of a child's quilt.

tools and techniques

chapter 1:
wear

One year at my daughter's birthday party, we made paper fairy wings for her friends to wear and take home. Later, one of the mothers told me that her daughter insisted on wearing her wings to bed! She assured her child that all fairies take off their wings to sleep at night. Many children make no distinction between dress-up clothes and regular clothes. One of the best things about childhood is being able to dress up in any crazy thing you like, and no one even blinks.

The projects in this chapter are perfect for children who appreciate some handmade whimsy in their wardrobe. The Insect Capes (page 28), Sew Sweet Strawberry Bag (page 36), and Instant Drama Chenille Duo (page 40) are great projects for beginning sewists and just right for getting started with kids. The construction may be simple, but the completed projects are full of whimsy and major dress-up (as well as everyday wear!) potential. In fact, both of my girls use a Sew Sweet Strawberry Bag to carry their snacks to school.

The Laugh at Yourself Slippers (page 32) require a little more sewing skill. They are ripe for variation, so don't be surprised when family members of all ages begin hinting about details for a pair of their own. I have been known to wear boa and slipper samples around the studio when I am cold. So go ahead, size up those slippers to fit you, throw on a boa. And if your friends laugh, well, then you know they want some, too!

MATERIALS

* ⅓ yd (30.5 cm) of 72" (183 cm) wide felt for insect wings

* 4 scraps of 4" × 4" (10 × 10 cm) felt for ladybug spots

* Coordinating thread

* Contrasting thread for beetle and grasshopper wings

* 24" (61 cm) of extra-wide double-fold bias tape

* 1 ⅞–1¼" (2.2–3.2 cm) button for the closure

or

* 22" (56 cm) of extra-wide double-fold bias tape and a ½" (1.3 cm) piece of sew-on Velcro for the closure

TOOLS

* Basic Sewing Kit

* Insect Capes patterns on side A of the insert

* Darning or free-motion foot for your sewing machine (optional)

FINISHED SIZE

Like their real-life counterparts, these wings vary in size. The ladybug wings are 26" × 23" (66 × 58.5 cm). The beetle wings are 25" × 22" (63.5 × 56 cm). The grass-hopper wings are 31" × 20" (79 × 51 cm).

Insect Capes

Made simply with felt, bias tape, and lovely stitching, these insect wings could almost be considered elegant. This project is very versatile. Enlarge or reduce the pattern to make capes for larger or smaller children. Make a bunch in a variety of colors and soon you will have a whole menagerie of beetles, grasshoppers, and ladybugs. Try a pair of Laugh at Yourself Slippers (page 32) in matching colors for an insect ensemble.

You can sew up the grasshopper and beetle wings without the detail stitching, but this is a great way to practice free-motion sewing before you tackle a bigger project. You can stitch on either a button closure or a Velcro closure. If you choose the button option, extra supervision during playtime is essential because it will not release quickly.

1 First cut two Ladybug, Beetle, or Grasshopper Wings (see pattern insert) from felt.

2 Add details on the wings. For the ladybug, cut a Large Spot and a Small Spot from black felt. Position the spots on the wings either using the markings on the pattern as a guide or placing them wherever you prefer. Make sure you pin the spots to create mirror images on the two wings. Machine- or hand-appliqué the spots onto the wings.

For the grasshopper and beetle capes, machine stitch the wing details in contrasting thread **(FIGURE 1)**. For the grasshopper, I started with a free-motion spiral, sewed scallops down the entire length of each wing, and then ended with a spiral. For the beetle, I sewed simple lines down the length of each wing. Try eyeballing this for a natural look.

3 Sew the neck. Decide if you'll use a button or a Velcro closure.

For a button closure, find the narrower side of the bias tape. With the wings right side up in front of you, start at the right neck corner of the right-hand wing. Tuck in the short end of the bias tape and pin the long edge to the front of the wings, matching the raw edge of the narrow side of the bias tape to the curved neck edge of the wings. Leave the rest of

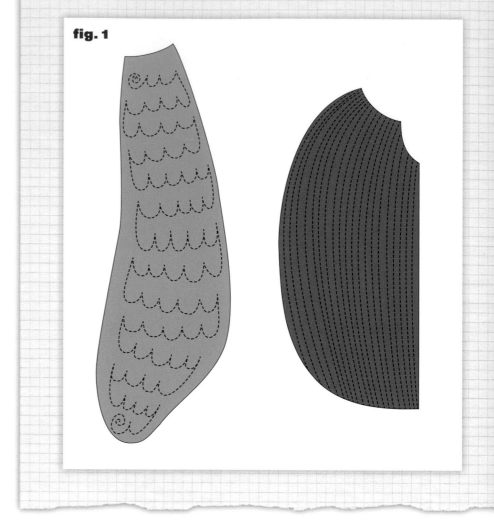

fig. 1

the bias tape free past the left-hand wing.

Stitch along the tape in the fold closest to the raw edge of the narrow side of the tape, attaching it to the wings. Then fold the bias tape over the neck edge.

Starting with the long free end of the bias tape, stitch the bias tape closed for 3" (7.5 cm). Raise your sewing machine foot, leaving the needle in the bias tape. Bring the free end of the bias tape around in a loop and tuck the end into the bias tape opening just in front of the needle. This

creates the loop for the button. You may want to clip the end at an angle.

Continue sewing down the long edge and over each wing. Last, sew a button on the top right corner of the right-hand wing.

For a quick-release Velcro closure, start by opening the bias tape and folding it in half widthwise to find the center. Find the narrower side of the bias tape. Pin the bias tape to the front of the wings with one wing on either side of the center, matching the raw edge of the narrow side of the bias tape to the curved neck edge of the wings.

Kid Work

★ Select the felt
★ Sew the spots on the ladybug wings

Stitch along the tape in the fold closest to the raw edge of the narrow
side of the tape, attaching it to the
wings. Fold the bias tape over the
neck edge and tuck in the ends of the
bias tape on both sides.

Then, stitch the opening closed on
the front starting with one short end,
continuing down the long edge, over
each wing, past the other side, and
turning to finish the other short edge.

Last, clip the corners of the two
Velcro pieces so they don't irritate
your little bug. Sew the Velcro on the
ends of the bias tape, positioning
them so that when they overlap, they
stick together.

MATERIALS

* ⅓–½ yd (30.5–45.5 cm) fabric for exterior, depending on the slipper size

* ⅓–½ yd (30.5–45.5 cm) fabric for lining, depending on the slipper size

* One 7" (10 cm) square of non-skid fabric such as Ultrasuede

* 16–32" (40.5–81.5 cm) of 16" (40.5 cm) wide batting

* Fabric scraps for tabs

* Coordinating thread

* Contrasting thread

* Two squares of Velcro or two 3" (7.5 cm) lengths of elastic or elastic hair bands

* Trims such as bells, felt balls, felt scraps for flowers, or buttons

* Embroidery floss for the leaves

TOOLS

* Basic Sewing Kit

* Laugh at Yourself Slippers patterns on side A of the insert

FINISHED SIZE

The size of your child's foot! Exact measurements will depend on the slipper size you are making.

Laugh at Yourself Slippers

I have always had a thing for crazy shoes, especially on kids. And when I see them on kids, I want a pair for myself! They're even more fun when you make them. These slippers are guaranteed to cause giggling. No matter what your children's mood, wearing silly slippers will make them feel better. Kids will love to help choose colors, fabrics, and all the giggle-causing embellishments. This is a perfect project for mining your child's imagination. Use the basic pattern for the base, choose a closure, and then go for it.

With flannel linings and soft quilting, they are as practical and comfortable as they are fun. The tab and elastic closures help the slippers stay on through playtime. Make a pair for every member of the family and beyond!

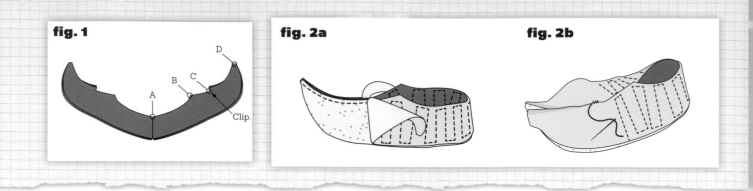

fig. 1

fig. 2a

fig. 2b

For the slipper uppers and soles, you can use whole cloth or piece your own fabric together for patchwork slippers. Experiment with the quilting—this is a great project to try out some fun stitching by hand or machine.

The instructions include two different closures: a tab with Velcro for opening and closing or an elastic band that is attached on both sides and will stretch and hold the slippers on snugly. You can use elastic sold in a package, but because you only need small amounts, try using elastic hair bands. They come in a rainbow of colors and a variety of sizes and textures.

For the nonskid bottoms, use Ultrasuede, leather scraps, or specialty nonskid fabric with little rubber dots. Try repurposing a jacket or handbag from the thrift store. If all else fails, get a squeeze bottle of fabric paint from the craft store and make dots on the soles of the slippers.

The best way to figure out the right size for your children's slippers isn't very scientific, but it works. Simply enlarge the pattern on your copier until it matches their feet!

1 The Sole pattern (see pattern insert) has a foot measuring line. Place your child's heel against the heel of the pattern. The toe should just hit the foot measuring line. Enlarge or reduce the Sole

pattern until it's the right size, noting the final percentage you use. Enlarge or reduce the other pattern pieces to the same percentage.

The patterns may seem big, but the extra length is for the turned-up toe and the seam allowances. If you know the slipper wearer's shoe size, you can print out a shoe size chart from the Internet and then enlarge or reduce the Sole pattern until the foot measuring line matches the correct size on the chart.

2 Cut four Slipper Uppers from the outside fabric, four from the batting, and four from the lining fabric. Make sure you have two outsides and linings facing one way and two facing the opposite way.

3 Cut two Soles from the outside fabric, two from the batting, and two from the lining fabric. Also cut two Small Sole Patches and two Large Sole Patches from nonskid fabric. The small ones will go on the heels, and the large ones will go on the ball of the foot.

Make the Uppers

4 First, make four stacks with the uppers. Layer the batting on the bottom, then the lining with right side facing up, and finally the outside fabric on the top with right side facing down. Make sure you have

two stacks facing one way and two stacks facing the opposite way.

5 Using the pattern, transfer points A, B, C, and D onto the top fabric of each stack. Sew the center upper seam on each of the four layered stacks from point A to point B and then from point B to point C. Clip the curves and the corner at point B. Make a scant ¼" (6 mm) clip at point C from the edge of the seam into the fabric just at the end of the stitching.

6 Match two sets of two uppers so they face in opposite directions. Open the heel of each side so the right side of the outside fabric and the right side of the lining fabric are facing up. Match the right sides together (outside fabric to outside fabric and lining to lining). Fold the batting toward the outside fabric on one side and toward the lining fabric on the other side to eliminate bulk. Sew the heel seam on each slipper. Trim the seam allowance of the batting close to the stitching.

7 Turn each piece so the right sides of the lining and the outside fabric are facing out and the batting is sandwiched between them. Smooth the curves and gently push out point B from the inside on each side. Press the uppers **(FIGURE 1)**.

8 Baste around the bottom edge of each upper to keep the layers from shifting during quilting. Hand- or machine-quilt each upper on the sides and heel of the slippers but keep away from the front. Refer to the pattern for the line where to stop quilting.

9 For each slipper, match the right sides of the outside fabric at the center upper seam. Fold the lining fabric out of the way and then sew the center upper seam from point C to point D. You are sewing the outside fabric and the batting from each side together but keeping the linings free **(FIGURE 2a)**

10 Fold the lining back on each side, tuck under the seam allowances, and handstitch the lining closed from point C to point D **(FIGURE 2b)**.

11 Finish quilting the rest of both slipper uppers.

Make the Soles

12 Layer the soles with the lining on the bottom, right side facing down, then add the batting and the outside fabric on top with right side facing up. Baste around the outside of each sole.

13 To add nonskid patches, position them on the outside fabric of each sole. Topstitch the patches to the soles. Hand- or machine-quilt the soles around the nonskid patches.

Make the Closure

You can use either Velcro or elastic to make a closure for the slippers.

14 **If using a tab and Velcro closure,** sew one side of each Velcro square to each upper where indicated on the pattern. Then cut four Tabs using the pattern.

Match two sets and, with right sides together, sew around three sides of each tab, leaving a short side open. Clip the corners and turn the tabs right sides out. Fold under the remaining side and press.

Sew the remaining side of the Velcro square onto the closed short end of the tab. Match the open end to the tab placement line on the slipper upper. Topstitch the tab onto the slipper, closing the open side at the same time.

If using elastic, start by sewing one end of the hair band or piece of elastic onto one side of the center upper slit. Sew the other end to the other side of the center upper slit. Repeat with the other slipper.

15 To make flowers, cut flower shapes from felt or wool using the pattern. Cut circles from felt for the centers. Sew the circles onto the flowers and sew a button or felt ball on top.

16 Sew a flower or a button onto the free end of each tab to cover the Velcro stitching or the ends of the elastic. To add leaves, cut a leaf shape from felt or wool. Using embroidery floss, sew the leaf onto the slipper with a backstitch.

Kid Work

★ Choose colors, fabrics, and trims
★ Assemble and sew embellishments

Assemble the Slippers

17 With the outside fabric together, pin the uppers to the soles, matching point D on the uppers to the toe on the sole and the center heel seam to the center back of the sole. Sew around the slippers.

18 Carefully trim the fabric and batting at point D close to the stitching. Do not trim or clip any other seam allowance.

19 Turn the slippers right side out, carefully easing out point D and finger pressing the seams. Add more silliness with bells or felt balls on the toes, funky buttons, or bright flowers!

MATERIALS

* ⅓ yd (30.5 cm) of cotton fabric, dupioni silk, or other medium-weight fabric for bag

* ⅓ yd (30.5 cm) of cotton quilting-weight fabric for lining

* Scrap of white felt or white cotton fabric for strawberry flower

* 66" (168 cm) of ⅜" (1 cm) wide green ribbon or rickrack for strawberry leaves

* Yellow button for strawberry flower

* 56" (142 cm) of ⅜" (1 cm) wide ribbon for drawstring

* Coordinating thread

* 32 seed beads, beading needle, and thread (optional)

TOOLS

* Basic Sewing Kit

* Sew Sweet Strawberry Bag pattern on side B of the insert

* Safety pin or bodkin

* Flower-shaped yo-yo maker (optional)

FINISHED SIZE

The strawberry-shaped bag is 9" × 6" (23 × 15 cm).

Sew Sweet Strawberry Bag

This lovely strawberry-shaped bag is a great project for beginners and quick enough to whip up as a special gift bag. Use polka-dot cotton for a yummy everyday version or try something fancier, like dupioni silk. Add a few beads and take it with you for a night out. Whatever materials you choose, give some attention to the lining. A fun lining fabric adds an extra bit of sweetness.

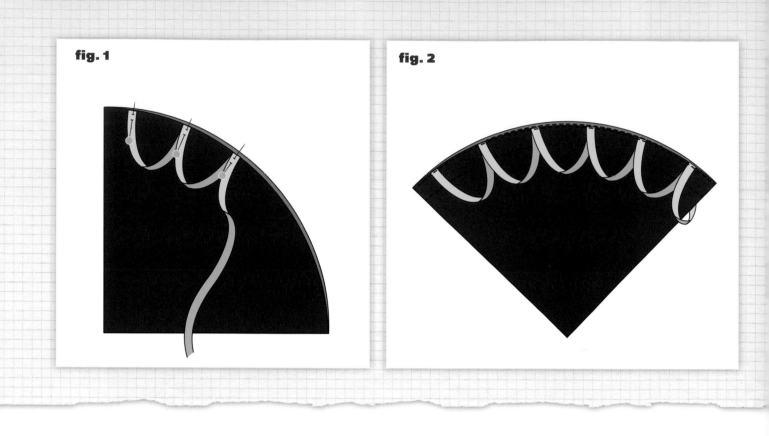

fig. 1

fig. 2

As with all of the projects in this book, use a ¼" (6 mm) seam allowance unless otherwise noted. You can make several of these bags at once by cutting and sewing them assembly line style—think party favors!

1 Using the Sew Sweet Strawberry Bag pattern (see insert), cut two Bag pieces from the outer fabric and two from the lining. Mark the two openings for the drawstring on the outer fabric and the opening for turning on the lining.

2 With the right sides of the two lining pieces together, sew the two straight side seams of the lining, turning the corner at the point and leaving the opening for turning as indicated on the pattern. Clip the point and turn the lining right side out. Press the seams open.

3 With right sides together, sew the two straight side seams on

the outer piece, turning the corner at the point and leaving openings for the drawstring as indicated on the pattern. Clip the point and turn the strawberry right side out. Press the seams open.

4 If using beads, sew them randomly onto the outer fabric, keeping away from the top edge where you will make the drawstring casing. Without knotting the thread, insert the needle through the wrong side of the fabric. Leave a tail hanging on the back, thread the bead onto the needle, and insert the needle back into the front of the fabric about ⅟₁₆" (2 mm) away from where it came up. Knot the two ends together on the back and trim to ½" (1.3 cm). Repeat for the remaining beads.

5 Stitch the strawberry leaves next. Mark the ribbon into twelve sections of 5½" (14 cm) each. Mark the spots for the ribbon loops

on both sides of the outer bag piece. Pin down one end of the ribbon at the first spot, matching the raw end of the ribbon to the fabric's raw edge. Fold the ribbon at the first spot on the ribbon and pin it to the next spot on the bag, matching the ribbon fold to the raw edge of the fabric. Continue in this manner all the way around the top of the strawberry until the end of the ribbon meets the beginning **(FIGURE 1)**.

6 Baste the ribbon-loop leaves onto the strawberry by sewing around the top of the strawberry, ⅛" (3 mm) from the edge.

7 Turn the outer strawberry piece with right sides facing on the inside. Pin the lining to the inside, right sides together and side seams matching. Make sure the loops are inside! Sew the lining to the bag, stitching around the top edges.

8 Turn the whole bag through the hole in the lining. Handsew the opening closed. Push the lining into the bag.

9 Press the top seam with a cool iron to avoid melting the ribbon. Topstitch around the edge of the bag ⅞" (2.2 cm) away from the top edge; this will make the channel for the drawstring. Be careful to keep the ribbon loops free.

10 Turn the ribbon down so the loops are against the outside body of the bag. Topstitch along the top edge of the bag, catching in the ribbon as you go **(FIGURE 2)**.

11 Cut the drawstring in half and seal the four ends if

necessary (see Tools and Techniques, page 19). Using a bodkin, thread the ribbon through one of the drawstring openings, continuing through the entire channel and coming back out through the same hole. Knot the ends together with an overhand knot. Do the same for the other drawstring through the opposite hole.

12 Last, make the flower. Trace around the Flower pattern on your scrap of white felt (or cotton fabric) and cut out one flower. Sew the yellow button in the center of the flower. Attach the flower near the top of the strawberry.

Alternatively, you could follow the manufacturer's directions for making a fabric yo-yo with a yo-yo maker. Use whichever side of the flower you prefer. (I like what they consider the back side!) Sew a yellow button in the center of the flower, then attach the flower near the top of the strawberry. Oh, so sweet!

MATERIALS

* ½ yd (45.5 cm) each of four different flannels (2 yd [1.8 m] total)

* 60" (152.5 cm) piece of ⅝" (1.5 cm) wide grosgrain or other sturdy ribbon

* Coordinating or contrasting thread

TOOLS

* Basic Sewing Kit

* Walking foot

FINISHED SIZE

The boa is a generous 4" × 60" (10 × 152.5 cm).

Instant Drama Chenille Boa

For my girls' birthdays, my friend Susan Borger designed these fabulous chenille boas. Surprisingly simple, this boa is made of bias-cut flannel. Throw it in the washer and dryer, and presto—the flannel becomes chenille. Make one for yourself and go dancing! You can even make Hazel Doll (page 112) her own Instant Drama Chenille Boa—totally silly, but you know you want to!

Safety alert: Supervision when playing with a boa is a must. Never let children play unattended with anything that goes around their necks.

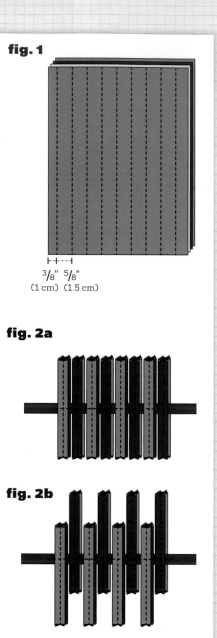

fig. 1

³/₈" ⁵/₈"
(1 cm) (1.5 cm)

fig. 2a

fig. 2b

For more chenille projects, check out the surface chenille and chenille grass in the Over in the Meadow Landscape Rug (page 68) and the mane and tail on Alexander Lion (page 122).

1 Cut the flannel into bias strips 8" (20.5 cm) wide. (See Tools and Techniques, page 24, for how to cut fabric on the bias.)

2 Make a continuous strip of each color by overlapping the short ends of each bias strip (the ends will be on the diagonal) about ½" (1.3 cm) with right sides up. Sew with a wide zigzag stitch.

3 Stack the four strips on top of each other, aligning the edges. Pin.

4 Starting on one long edge and using the walking foot attachment for your sewing machine, sew the entire length of the stack of flannel together ³/₈" (1 cm) from the edge. Then sew subsequent rows ⁵/₈" (1.5 cm) from the one before it **(FIGURE 1)**. Continue until the entire stack of flannels is sewn. If your walking foot does not have a stitch guide to help sew the ⁵/₈" (1.5 cm) rows, mark the rows before you sew. You can also eyeball the rows—chenille is very forgiving!

5 Cut the long, stitched stack widthwise into 6" (15 cm) sections.

6 Cut between the stitched rows, making ⁵/₈" × 6" (1.5 × 15 cm) strips. You should have about 150 strips. It's okay if you have fewer; your boa will just be shorter.

7 Assemble the boa by sewing the flannel strips to the ribbon. Starting 2" (5 cm) in from one end of the ribbon, place one flannel strip

You'll use your washer and dryer to make the boa fluffy and dramatic. Washing and drying will cause the edges of the flannel to fray, but because you cut it on the bias, it will not unravel. I used a regular warm water and extra-high-spin wash cycle and regular hot dry cycle. Add a towel or two for friction.

Kid Work

★ Choose the fabrics
★ Sew the strips onto the ribbon
★ Hand strips to the sewist
★ Take charge of washing and drying the boa

perpendicular and under the ribbon and one strip perpendicular and on top of the ribbon. The center of the strip should match the center of the ribbon. Start sewing straight down the middle of the ribbon, adding adjacent strips under and on top of the ribbon as you go **(FIGURE 2a)**.

You can alternate which side of the strip is up, if you like. Or, shift the flannel strips sideways so there are 2" (5 cm) or so on one side of the ribbon and 4" (10 cm) on the other **(FIGURE 2b)**. Alternate as you go. By shifting the strips, the shorter 2" (5 cm) sections will make the boa fuller near the ribbon—just a different look!

8 Add strips until you are 2" (5 cm) from the end of the ribbon. If you run out of strips before then, trim the ribbon. Seal the two ribbon ends or sew a small hem.

9 Now the magic happens! Throw your boa into the washer and dryer. You may need to repeat this step several times to achieve the desired fluff. Voilà!

Stunning Chenille for Every Project

by Susan Borger

Susan Borger is a fabulous textile designer who taught me everything I know about sewing with chenille. She has fantastic tips for making wonderful chenille for any type of project.

Flannel is my choice of fabric for chenille projects. An inexpensive, loosely woven, 100 percent cotton flannel is the best choice for achieving more fluff and dimensionality. A better made, more expensive, tightly woven flannel will not shrink or ruffle as much and won't be as dimensional. You want woolly caterpillars, not flattened earthworms!

Remember, too, when selecting flannel fabric that a printed fabric often has a white back side or a lighter background color on the back.

Whether you stack the fabric to make independent chenille strips, like for the Instant Drama Chenille Boa (page 40) or Alexander Lion (page 122), or stitch the stacked fabric onto a base fabric, as with one of the special patches in the Over in the Meadow Landscape Rug (page 68), washing and drying will cause the flannel to shrink and fluff up, exposing more of the white or light background color. That will not happen with yarn-dyed fabrics unless you deliberately stack contrasting colors.

To best control how the colors will look, it's a good idea to test your fabric before you plunge ahead with a full-scale chenille project. Cutting on the grain, cut 5" (12.5 cm) squares from all your fabric options. Then stack them in different orders, stitch channels on the bias, and cut through the top layers between your rows of stitching. Leave the bottom layer intact as your base. Wash and dry this stack and you'll see exactly how your different flannels will look when they're turned into chenille. You can use these as samples for planning your project. If you like surprises, don't bother with the 5" (12.5 cm) test squares.

The number of layers in your project will also determine how much dimension you ultimately get. Varying the number of layers in your test squares can be beneficial for predicting or controlling the fluffiness of the chenille.

A word of warning, though. Sometimes it becomes difficult to determine the straight grain of the fabric once the selvedges are gone. For the chenille process to succeed, you need to stitch on the bias and cut between the rows of stitched channels on the bias. When you stitch on the bias, you are locking the fibers down where they cross at angles, making it difficult for the fibers to ravel. Raveling is not desired in this process.

And, finally, do check your dryer's lint trap frequently during the drying process. It can fill up quickly with the fuzzy-surfaced flannel!

Chenille adds wonderful texture and is especially welcome when making projects for kids. They love the softness and fun it brings. Be sure to have them help with the washing and ironing so they can see the magic happen!

chapter 2:
play

Even when I was young, my idea of play was making things. In our family room, my mother stacked ice cream tubs full of fabric on the shelves, along with paper and scissors and glue and trims. Her sewing machine was on a desk, and my father made a big round table for the middle of the room for working on projects. With a workspace that's just as inviting to your children, you can double the play in your home.

The projects in this chapter are launch pads for imaginative play as well as inspired sewing. There are many ways you can make these your own in the creating as well as in the playing. The projects are adaptable, flexible, and have the potential to turn your children into designers as well as sewists.

With the Quilted Dollhouse (page 46) and the Indoor Snowman (page 62), you handle the serious sewing while your kids create the accessories that make them such special playthings.

These projects encourage you to indulge your own inner child as well. Once I got started with the extravaganza of the Over in the Meadow Landscape Rug (page 68), it was so much fun I didn't want to stop. I would have made it

as big as a room, but—oh right— I had kids to take care of and other projects to make. For the Topsy-Turvy Story Quilt (page 56) your children's drawings take center stage, creating an arena for their imagination. With both of these projects, you get to collaborate with your children to create a whole new world for them to play in.

MATERIALS

* ½ yd (45.5 cm) of fabric for roof

* ½ yd (45.5 cm) of fabric for roof underside

* ½ yd (45.5 cm) of fabric for exterior walls and exterior wall filler

* ½ yd (45.5 cm) of fabric for interior walls

* ½ yd (45.5 cm) of fabric for main floor

* ½ yd (45.5 cm) of fabric for main floor underside

* ¼ yd (23 cm) of fabric for garden extension

* ½ yd (45.5 cm) of fabric for second floor

* ½ yd (45.5 cm) of fabric for second floor underside

* Two different ½ yd (45.5 cm) pieces of fabric for extra floor

* ¼ yd (23 cm) of fabric for loft

* ¼ yd (23 cm) of fabric for loft underside

* Coordinating thread

* Contrasting thread

* Embroidery floss

* 3½ yd (3.2 m) of 20" (51 cm) wide interfacing

* 3½ yd (3.2 m) of batting at least 14" (35.5 cm) wide

* 14 yd (12.8 m) of sewable boning

* 1 yd (91.5 cm) of ⅞" (2.2 cm) wide ribbon for handle and second floor support

* 1½ yd (1.4 m) extra-wide double-fold bias tape for window and skylight binding

----

continued on next page ☞

Quilted Dollhouse

A dollhouse is a staple of child's play. With wonderful fabrics and kid-made dolls and furniture, the Quilted Dollhouse is extra special. A few integrated features turn this dollhouse into a flexible, modern living arrangement. Your child can change the scenery behind the dollhouse by hanging her drawings on the outside facing in.

For a special touch, embellish the house with an appliqué or embroidery designed by your child. Some flowers on the exterior, a chandelier on the ceiling, or a dresser on an interior wall personalize this project.

When your child is ready to close up the house, she can store her dolls and furniture inside. Make sure the second floor is up inside the house, fold up the main floor, and then fold down the roof, looping the elastic over the lower button. Then pull the ribbon handle through the skylight for easy carrying. If you are making the Quilted Dollhouse as a surprise, include a box of supplies for the lucky recipient to make her own dolls and furniture.

* 3" (7.5 cm) length of elastic or elastic hair band and one ½" (1.3 cm) button

* 6" (15 cm) piece of Velcro

* Four ⅜" (1 cm) buttons with shank

* 14" (35.5 cm) thin dowel for second floor support

* ¼ yd (45.5 cm) of fabric for exterior wall design (optional)

* ¼ yd (23 cm) of fabric for loft wall (optional)

* Printable fabric (optional)

TOOLS
* Basic Sewing Kit

* Walking foot and zipper foot

* Child's drawings for embroidery on the house

* Compass

FINISHED SIZE
When all folded up, the Quilted Dollhouse is 11" × 14" × 11" (28 × 35.5 × 28 cm).

The Quilted Dollhouse is all straight lines and angles to cut and sew. The cutting chart divides the dollhouse into six sections: the main floor, the second floor, an extra floor, the roof, three walls, and a loft. For the main floor, roof, walls, and loft, the fabrics are cut in larger pieces and sewn into envelopes to make several planes at once. The interfacing and batting pieces are slid into the fabric envelopes and stitched in between to form the corners and angles. The second floor and extra floor are each made as a single plane.

This is a fabric dollhouse made from cotton quilting-weight fabric, so it will naturally be soft and bendable. To give the dollhouse some structure, each piece of interfacing is framed with boning. I used polyester boning without a fabric covering, but you could use covered boning, as long as it's very rigid. You can sew right over it when you machine-quilt the sections. The only additional support is provided by the ribbon channel and wood dowel used for the second floor. If it is too relaxed for your taste, you can add more ribbon and dowel supports on other sections of the house.

As you construct the house, make sure any embellishments, like pictures and embroideries, are oriented correctly. If you are like me and need to see how the whole house is coming together before you commit to the details, you can embroider the designs after each section is made but before the house is assembled. Keep in mind that the sewing will be trickier if you do it this way. You will need to keep the needle and floss between the layers so the stitches will not show on the other side of the section.

1 Choose your fabrics. The cutting chart assumes that you use a different piece of cotton quilting-weight fabric for each part and plane of the house. Go all out when picking your fabrics! Find the fabric that resembles the wallpaper you love and the siding that would shock your neighbors. Take advantage of the opportunity to make it the house that you have always wanted!

2 Cut fabric, batting, and interfacing according to the cutting chart (FIGURE 1), keeping track of the sections that go together. For the angled piecing on the Main Floor section and the angle of the Second Floor piece, follow the cutting chart first and then refer to FIGURE 2 to cut the angles.

3 Add structure to the dollhouse by framing each piece of interfacing with boning. You have twelve pieces of cut interfacing, one for each plane of the house. Keep the boning in one long piece. Match one end of the boning to one side of the first piece of interfacing. Use a zigzag stitch to sew down the boning until you get to the edge of the interfacing, then cut the boning flush with the side of the interfacing. Turn the interfacing 90 degrees and sew the boning down the next side. Continue on the two remaining sides of the interfacing.

Repeat with the other eleven pieces of interfacing (FIGURE 3).

4 Match all of the interfacing pieces with the corresponding pieces of batting. With the boning side toward the batting, line the pieces up and press them together with your hand.

5 If you plan to embroider some of your child's drawings on the house, copy them to the appropriate size and transfer them onto the fabric where you would like them. (See Tools and Techniques, page 16.)

fig. 1

SECTION	FABRIC	BATTING	INTERFACING
Walls	Cut 1 Exterior Wall: 11½" × 28¼" (29 × 72 cm) Cut 1 Exterior Wall filler: 2½" × 11½" (6.5 × 29 cm) Cut 1 Exterior Accent Wall: 6¾" × 11½" (17 × 29 cm) Cut 1 Interior Wall: 11½" × 30½" (29 × 77.5 cm) Cut 1 Interior Loft Wall: 6½" × 11½" (16.5 × 29 cm)	Cut 2: 10¾" × 10¾" (27.5 × 27.5 cm) Cut 1: 10¾" × 13¾" (27.5 × 35 cm)	Cut 2: 10¾" × 10¾" (27.5 × 27.5 cm) Cut 1: 10¾" × 13¾" (27.5 × 35 cm)
Main Floor	Cut 1 Main Floor: 14½" × 28" (37 × 71 cm) Cut 1 Main Floor Underside: 14½" × 28" (37 × 71 cm) Cut 1 Main Floor Garden Extension: 11½" × 14½" (29 × 37 cm)	Cut 2: 10¾" × 13¾" (27.5 × 35 cm) Cut 1: 5¼" × 13¾" (13.5 × 35 cm)	Cut 2: 10¾" × 13¾" (27.5 × 35 cm) Cut 1: 5¼" × 13¾" (13.5 × 35 cm)
Second Floor	Cut 1 Second Floor: 11½" × 14½" (29 × 37 cm) Cut 1 Second Floor Underside: 11½" × 14½" (29 × 37 cm) Cut 2 Tabs: 2¾" × 7½" (7 × 19 cm)	Cut 1: 10¾" × 13¾" (27.5 × 35 cm)	Cut 1: 10¾" × 13¾" (27.5 × 35 cm)
Extra Floor	Cut 1 Extra Floor, fabric (A): 11½" × 14½" (29 × 37 cm) Cut 1 Extra Floor, fabric (B): 11½" × 14½" (29 × 37 cm)	Cut 1: 10¾" × 13¾" (27.5 × 35 cm)	Cut 1: 10¾" × 13¾" (27.5 × 35 cm)
Roof	Cut 1 Roof: 11½" × 22½" (29 × 57 cm) Cut 1 Roof Underside: 11½" × 22½" (29 × 57 cm)	Cut 1: 10¾" × 13¾" (27.5 × 35 cm) Cut 1: 7¾" × 10¾" (19.5 × 27.5 cm)	Cut 1: 10¾" × 13¾" (27.5 × 35 cm) Cut 1: 7¾" × 10¾" (19.5 × 27.5 cm)
Loft	Cut 1 Loft: 6½" × 8" (16.5 × 20.5 cm) Cut 1 Loft Underside: 6½" × 8" (16.5 × 20.5 cm)	Cut 1: 4¾" × 5¾" (12 × 14.5 cm) Cut 1: 2¼" × 5¾" (5.5 × 14.5 cm)	Cut 1: 4¾" × 5¾" (12 × 14.5 cm) Cut 1: 2¼" × 5¾" (5.5 × 14.5 cm)

Consider details that would be difficult to make as 3-D elements, such as flowers on an outside wall and a lamp on the ceiling. Embroider the designs.

6 In my dollhouse, I also included a picture for the loft wall. Shrink your child's drawing to fit the house; mine is 25% the size of the original drawing. Next, use your computer printer to print the drawing onto printable fabric. Cut out the picture, fold under ⅛" (3 mm) all around, and appliqué it onto the house. You can even embroider a frame around the edge.

Make the House Sections

7 Start with the three walls, which you make all at the same time. Piece together the fabrics for the loft wall and the exterior walls, following the wall-piecing diagram **(FIGURE 4)**. The exterior wall is made of three sections: the Exterior Wall, the Exterior Accent Wall, and the Exterior Wall Filler. The interior wall is made of two sections: the Interior Wall and the Interior Loft Wall.

8 With right sides together, sew the two long sides and one short side, creating a pocket. Clip the corners and turn right sides out. Press.

Measure 11" (28 cm) in from the short sewn side and mark a topstitching line parallel to the short side. Measure 14" (35.5 cm) from that first line and mark another topstitching line. The topstitching will make the three pockets for the three walls, and the topstitched lines will be the house corners.

9 Slide a square section of wall-sized interfacing and batting into the pocket and ease two of the

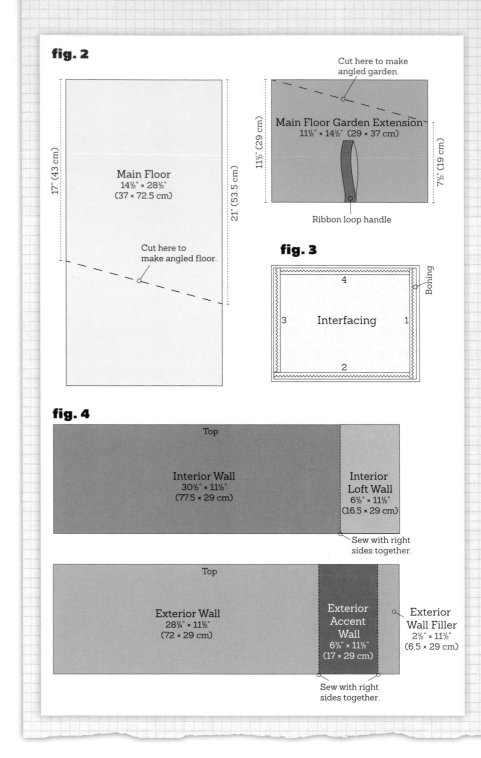

fig. 2

Main Floor
14½" × 28½"
(37 × 72.5 cm)

17" (43 cm)

21" (53.5 cm)

Cut here to make angled floor.

Cut here to make angled garden.

Main Floor Garden Extension
11½" × 14½" (29 × 37 cm)

11½" (29 cm)

7½" (19 cm)

Ribbon loop handle

fig. 3

Interfacing

Boning

3   1

4

2

fig. 4

Top

Interior Wall
30½" × 11½"
(77.5 × 29 cm)

Interior Loft Wall
6½" × 11½"
(16.5 × 29 cm)

Sew with right sides together.

Top

Exterior Wall
28¾" × 11½"
(72 × 29 cm)

Exterior Accent Wall
6¾" × 11½"
(17 × 29 cm)

Exterior Wall Filler
2½" × 11½"
(6.5 × 29 cm)

Sew with right sides together.

corners into the sewn corners of the pocket. Make sure the batting side faces the exterior wall. Topstitch across the pocket on the first marked line. A zipper foot makes it easy to sew next to the interfacing.

10 Slide the rectangular section of interfacing and batting into the wall pocket and topstitch on the second marked line. Slide in the remaining square section of interfacing and batting. Fold in

the raw edges of the pocket, tucking them around the last section of interfacing, and handsew or machine topstitch closed. You should now have three walls stitched in one piece.

11 Machine quilt the walls. My dollhouse has stripes quilted perpendicular to the stripes on the exterior fabric. All of my quilting is simple stripes and geometric grids in matching thread colors. Choose a quilting pattern that is appropriate for your fabric. If you have chosen solids or more subdued fabrics, use the quilting as a bolder design element. Use contrasting thread for added interest if desired.

Outline any embroidery you have done, or write the house address or name of the dollhouse family with free-motion quilting. Remember to consider both sides of the section and how the quilting will look with each fabric.

12 Add a window to the back wall of the house, which is the 11" × 14" (28 × 35.5 cm) section.

Measure 2½" (6.5 cm) in from all of the edges and draw a rectangle in the wall. Cut out the rectangle through the fabric, batting, and interfacing.

Bind the window by cutting 37" (94 cm) of bias tape and handsew it around the window to enclose the raw edge. The inside corners are impossible to get into with a sewing machine! You will need to clip the bias tape when you get to the interior corners (**FIGURE 5**, page 53). Overlap the ends where they meet, tucking in the raw edges.

13 You can make a system for hanging your child's scenery drawings behind the house. Sew two small shank buttons on the top two corners of the window, then hang a drawing (punch two holes in the top corners) to peek in through the opening.

14 Sew the main floor. Again, sew one large pocket with topstitching lines to create three planes. One 11" × 14" (28 × 35.5 cm) plane becomes the floor inside

the house, the other 11" × 14" (28 × 35.5 cm) plane becomes the garden that extends outside the house, and the 5½" × 14" (14 × 35.5 cm) extension becomes the flap that folds on top of the house for storage.

With right sides together, sew the two angled Interior Floor pieces together to form a rectangle. Lay the Interior Floor piece in front of you with right side up. Cut a 12" (30.5 cm) piece of ribbon, then fold it in half widthwise so the raw short edges are matching. Match the raw short edges of the ribbon loop to the raw edge of the Garden Extension, creating the dollhouse's handle (**FIGURE 2**). Then place the Exterior Floor piece right side down on top of the Interior Floor pieces. Sew the two long sides and the short side with the ribbon, creating a new pocket. Clip the corners and turn with fabric right sides out. Press.

15 Measure 5½" (14 cm) in from the short sewn side and mark a topstitching line. Measure 11" (28 cm) from the first line and mark a second topstitching line.

and batting into the pocket, keeping the batting toward the exterior fabric. Ease two of the corners into the sewn corners of the pocket. Topstitch on the marked line. Slide the remaining section of roof interfacing into the pocket. Fold in the raw edges of the pocket, tucking them around the last section of interfacing, and handsew or machine topstitch it closed.

20 Machine-quilt the roof. On my dollhouse roof, I quilted straight lines unevenly spaced. You may want to make a grid or scallops for shingles or go an entirely different direction with flowers on the roof.

21 The next step is to make a skylight that also serves as the hole for the carrying handle. Find the center of the larger roof section by measuring 7" (18 cm) in from one of the short sides and mark a parallel line with pins. Measure 5½" (14 cm) in from one of the long sides and mark a parallel line. The center of the roof is where the pins intersect. With a compass, draw a 3" (7.5 cm) diameter circle on the roof, and then cut it out.

22 Bind the skylight with bias tape. Cut 13" (33 cm) of bias tape and handsew it around the circle, overlapping the ends where they meet and tucking in the raw edges.

23 Now, make the loft. Match the two Loft pieces with the right sides together. Sew the two long sides and one short side, making another pocket. Clip the corners and turn fabric right sides out. Press.

Measure 5" (12.5 cm) in from the short sewn side and mark a topstitching line.

24 Slide the larger Loft section of interfacing and batting into the pocket, keeping the batting

16 Slide the narrow rectangle section of interfacing and batting into the pocket, keeping the batting toward the interior fabric. Ease two of the corners into the sewn corners of the pocket. Topstitch across the pocket at the first marked line. Slide one large rectangular section of interfacing and batting in next and topstitch on the next line. Slide in the remaining rectangular section. Fold in the raw edges of the pocket, tucking them around the last section of interfacing and handsew or machine topstitch it closed.

17 Machine-quilt the main floor. On my dollhouse, I quilted a geometric pattern to echo the black-and-white fabric. Tie the garden extension with floss instead of quilting it to add texture that mimics plants.

18 Make the roof next, sewing one pocket for several planes. Make two planes, one that is 11" × 14" (28 × 35.5 cm) and one that is 11" × 8" (28 × 20.5 cm). Lay the Exterior Roof piece down with the right side up. Fold the elastic in half and pin the loop in the middle of one short side, raw edges matching. Place the interior fabric with right side down on top of the elastic loop. Sew the two long sides and the short side with the elastic loop, making a new pocket. Clip the corners and turn with fabric right sides out. Press.

Measure 8" (20.5 cm) in from the short sewn side and mark a topstitching line. This will create the roof peak.

19 Slide the smaller of the two Roof sections of interfacing

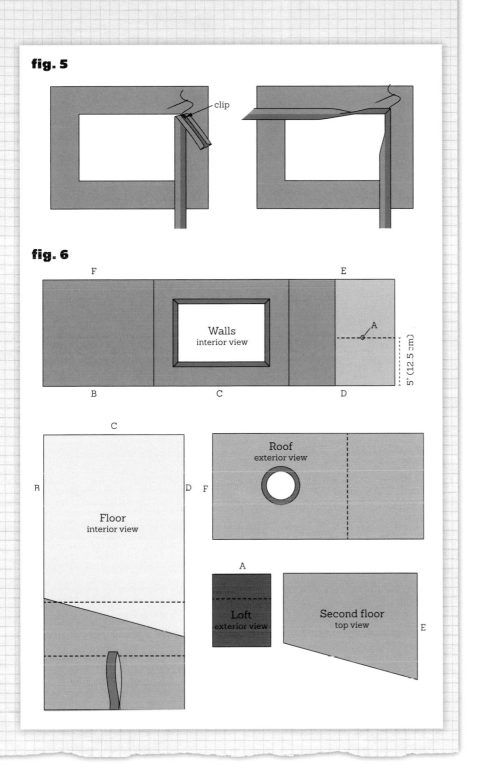

fig. 5

clip

fig. 6

F

E

Walls
interior view

A

5" (12.5 cm)

B

C

D

C

Floor
interior view

B

D

Roof
exterior view

F

A

Loft
exterior view

Second floor
top view

E

interfacing and handsew or machine topstitch closed.

25 Machine-quilt the loft to finish it. I used simple stripes and added whimsy with a printed fabric picture and embroidered frame, but this is a great little space to go all out with the quilting.

26 Now stitch a support to hold up the second floor. Make a Velcro tab by matching the two Tab pieces with right sides together. Sew around the two short sides and one long side of the tab. Clip the corners and turn right side out. Press.

27 To make the second floor, match the two pieces with right sides together. To cut the angle for the second floor, follow the angle for the Main Floor Garden Extension (**FIGURE 2**, page 50). Cut the angle on both Second Floor pieces at the same time. Cut the second floor batting and interfacing also at the same angle. Sew the two long sides.

Slip the support tab in between the floor fabrics and match the open side of the tab with the raw edges of the short side of the second floor. Sew the short side. Clip the corners and turn fabric right sides out. Press. Now you have a pocket with a tab.

Sew a 6" (15 cm) strip of one side of Velcro onto the tab right up next to the floor.

28 Slide the Second Floor section of interfacing and batting into the pocket and ease the corners into the sewn corners of the pocket. Fold in the raw edges of the pocket, tucking them around the last section of interfacing and handsew or machine topstitch closed.

29 Machine-quilt the second floor. Remember that it

toward the exterior fabric. Ease two of the corners into the sewn corners of the pocket. Topstitch on the marked line. Slide the remaining

section of loft interfacing and batting into the pocket. Fold in the raw edges of the pocket, tucking them around the last section of

can be flipped over to the side of the dollhouse and that the underside of the floor will be on the outside.

30 You can use the second floor as it is, but be aware that it will sag slightly. To add more structure, cut a piece of ribbon 14" (35.5 cm) long. Pin it down the center of the length on the ceiling side of the second floor. Topstitch the ribbon on both long sides to form a channel. Insert the dowel into one of the open short ends of the ribbon channel.

31 The extra floor is a single 11" × 14" (28 × 35.5 cm) plane. Two different and carefully chosen fabrics, one for each side, make this a very useful and easy addition. Slide the extra floor under the loft and on top of the main floor for a change in floor design. Use it outside the house for a patio or a pool. When your child is ready to close up the house after playing, slip the extra floor down the wall inside the window to keep the stored furniture and dolls inside.

Match the two pieces with right sides together. Sew the two long sides and one short side, making a pocket. Clip the corners and turn fabric right sides out. Press.

Slide the corresponding piece of interfacing and batting into the pocket and ease two of the corners into the sewn corners of the pocket. Fold in the raw edges of the pocket, tucking them around the last section of interfacing, and handsew or machine topstitch closed.

Machine-quilt the extra floor, paying attention to both sides of the floor.

32 Stand up the walls and pin the second floor into place. Hold it level with the Velcro tab hanging beneath it against the adjacent wall. Mark the area where the Velcro meets the wall and stitch down the other side of the Velcro.

33 If you waited to add the embroidered details, do so now. If you have already embroidered the details, see if there is anything else you want to add. You can even pin the sections together to see how your dollhouse will look.

Assemble the Dollhouse

34 Now build your house! Following **FIGURE 6** (page 53), assemble the house sections by matching the letters: A to A, B to B, and so on. Sew them together by hand. I used an invisible ladder stitch (see Tools and Techniques, page 20). The four sides of each section have a fabric fold from one side, the machine-stitched seam, and then the fabric fold from the other side. When handsewing the dollhouse sections with the invisible ladder stitch, I like to catch in the fold of the exterior fabric for a tidier look. There is no need to sew through the interfacing and boning.

Start by sewing the loft to the wall, then sew the walls to the floor. Next add the second floor to the walls. Finally, sew the roof to the walls. The extra floor remains separate and does not get sewn to the main house.

35 To support the roof, sew two shank buttons on the top two corners of the exterior wall for

Kid Work

★ Draw pictures for embroidery

★ Create scenery drawings

★ Choose fabrics and colors

★ Sew the straight sides on the house sections

★ Make the dolls and furniture

the roof edge to rest on. I used buttons covered with the same fabric as the exterior walls.

36 Lay the roof down so the larger section is parallel to the floor and the smaller section hangs down against the outside wall. Mark where the elastic loop falls on the exterior wall and sew a button on that mark. Plan ahead and situate an appropriate embroidery stitch where the button will be. On my dollhouse, the button is the center of a flower. Loop the elastic around the button to hold down the roof when the house is closed.

To close the house up after playing, slide the extra floor down inside the house against the large window wall. Make sure the second floor is up and held in place with Velcro. Fold up the main floor so the ribbon loop handle is on top of the house. Lay down the roof so the larger section is on top of the house and the smaller section is hanging down against the outside wall. Loop the elastic around the button. Pull the ribbon handle through the skylight, and off you go.

Outfitting the Quilted Dollhouse

Of course you could purchase dolls and dollhouse furniture for the Quilted Dollhouse, but we all know that making your own is the fun part. Certainly your creative child will want to do the same. I admit to getting completely sucked in when my daughters make these dolls and creating some myself. Joy! Projects for Sewing Space Interlopers (page 11) describes how kids can make little people from wooden doll pins, which are the perfect size for the Quilted Dollhouse. Your kids can whip up a whole bunch to use as an audience for a show or a crowd for a party. They are sure to also make a few favorites as permanent residents.

Embrace a "let them at it" attitude for making furniture and accessories for the Quilted Dollhouse. Supply your kids with glue, tape, and scissors. Save your empty thread spools of all shapes and sizes for the supply box. Small jewelry boxes, tiny containers, cardboard, and paper will be quickly transformed into furniture with glue, paint, and colored pencils.

At my house, we are fortunate to have Grandpa Adam, who makes furniture, supply us with scraps of wood. A few little blocks for chairs or some odd shapes to get the imagination going can add lots of options. If you don't have your own woodworking grandpa, check out your local hardware store or woodworking shop and ask about their scraps. The wood section at the craft store may also have wood parts that are useful. Of course, felt and fabric scraps, buttons, sequins, and other trims can be combined to make fun and funky dollhouse furniture.

Consider what materials your kids like to use and their abilities: a beginning knitter can knit a swatch for a rug, while a very young child can draw on a piece of paper and practice scissors skills by cutting fringe on the edges. This project can be a never-ending outlet for imagination—a family moves away and a new family moves in, new furniture is always welcome for redecorating, or your kids can make a car or a pet! You could even gently suggest they transform the whole thing into a store!

MATERIALS

* 2 yd (1.8 m) of light-colored cotton fabric wider than 68" (173 cm) or 4 yd (3.7 m) of 40" (101.5 cm) wide cotton fabric for day side

* 2 yd (1.8 m) of dark-colored cotton fabric wider than 68" (173 cm) or 4 yd (3.7 m) of 40" (101.5 cm) wide cotton fabric for night side

* Fabric scraps for appliqués

* Coordinating thread

* Contrasting thread

* 72" (183 cm) square of batting

* 6¼ yd (5.7 m) of extra-wide double-fold bias tape for binding

* White embroidery floss or pearl cotton for tying the quilt

* Buttons, ribbons, and other trims as desired

TOOLS

* Basic Sewing Kit

* Free-motion foot

* Child's drawings for appliqués

FINISHED SIZE

This quilt is 70" (178 cm) in diameter—big enough for several children to play with together, but small enough to take with you.

Topsy-Turvy Story Quilt

Circle quilts are wonderful for playing. Their shape alone invites children in and encourages gathering. This circle quilt is reversible: one side is day, and the other side is night. Both sides use your children's drawings to create inventive scenes straight from their imaginations. Children can use the scenes as settings for dramatic play, flipping the quilt back and forth as the story unfolds.

The fun begins with choosing images and fabrics and designing the composition. Get the kids involved, and your only job will be the appliqué. Straight-stitch machine appliqué is a quick and casual way to get it done so the adventure can begin.

This project really showcases your children's artwork. Pick and choose elements from different drawings and even from different kids to build your day and night scenes. You're creating a setting for telling stories, so choose elements of different sizes and in a variety of colors and shapes, such as a large orange sun and small red ladybug. This will add more interest to your composition and give you options to play with as you perfect your design.

It's okay to simplify your child's drawings if it makes for a better quilt design. Choose fabrics that highlight the features, like a camouflage print for a turtle's shell or a brown swirl for the bark of a tree. Kids will love to help sort through your scraps and stash looking for just the right fabric. They may even be inspired to improvise new images.

This quilt is designed to have a whole-cloth background for both the day and night sides, but you can piece it if you prefer. If you use fabric wider than 70" (173 cm), such as 90" (228.5 cm) or 108" (274 cm) wide, then the backgrounds can be one whole piece. If your fabric is narrower, you can piece them in two sections.

1 Piece both backgrounds if you're using narrower fabric.

Cut the length of fabric in half widthwise so you have two 2 yd (1.8 m) sections for each side. Match the two lengths of fabric with right sides together. Sew together down one long side using a 1" (2.5 cm) seam allowance. Trim the seam to ½" (1.3 cm), cutting off the selvedge, and then press the seam open.

2 Cut the day background fabric into a circle. With the fabric

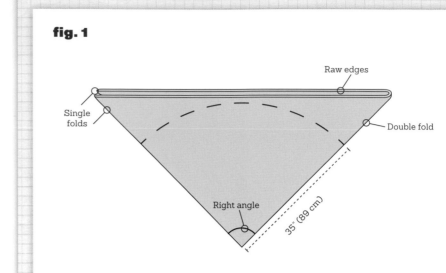

fig. 1

Raw edges

Single folds

Double fold

Right angle

35" (89 cm)

in a single layer, bring the lower left corner of the fabric diagonally up to the upper right-hand edge to make a triangle. You may have extra fabric on the side, depending on the width of your fabric, which you should trim off.

3 Bring the lower right-hand corner diagonally up to the upper left corner to fold the original triangle in half. You now have a right triangle. Using either a tape measure or a yardstick, measure 35" (89 cm) from the right angle point up toward the raw edges of the fabric. This will create an arc from one acute angle of the triangle to the other acute angle of the triangle **(FIGURE 1)**.

4 Match one end of the measuring tool to the point and move the other end in an arc, making a mark every few inches. Ask a kid to help hold the tape measure or yardstick. This is a great opportunity to sneak in some math ideas! Talk to your kid about radius, diameter, circumference, and fractions.

5 Cut the arc through all four layers of fabric. Open the fabric to reveal your lovely circle.

Repeat these steps with both the night background fabric and the batting.

6 On both fabric circles, machine stitch a scant ¼" (6 mm) around each circle. This will help keep the bias edges from stretching out of shape.

7 Assemble your child's day and night drawings. Enlarge or reduce them to create the scenes you and your child are imagining. You may need to adjust the sizes as you go. What looks like a good size coming out of the copier may appear small and insignificant on your quilt. Have extra images to play around with. Cut the paper images out. Kids can help with this also. Even though cutting fabric can be difficult for some children, the paper images can be cut by even young ones.

Kid Work

★ Create artwork for day and night scenes

★ Choose colors and fabrics

★ Cut out paper and fabric

★ Lay out the compositions

★ Finish the quilt with tying

8 Lay out the fabric circles and arrange the paper images on top, rearranging the images until it looks the way you want. Remove the images that aren't working and save them for another project. Get the kids involved in the composition. Remember to move elements in at least ½" (1.3 cm) from the edge so they are not covered by the binding.

9 Remove the paper images individually and use them as templates to cut the shapes from your fabric scraps. You can simplify the images by combining parts into one unit or add more interest by cutting different parts of an image from different fabrics. Use ribbons for stems or other thin lines or plan to embroider them later on.

If you feel your children can help with the fabric cutting, then by all means, let them help. Ease them into the process with simple shapes and remind them to cut from the edge of the fabric, not the middle!

10 Replace the paper images with the fabric appliqués as you go, making any adjustments in color, size, and composition as needed. When you and your children are satisfied with the quilt, take a photo or make notes on where the images go.

11 Remove all of the fabric cutouts. Starting in the center of one side of the quilt, appliqué one fabric image to the background at a time. Follow your photo or notes and work your way outward.

You can hand- or machine-appliqué this quilt. I appliquéd the quilt shown here with straight-stitch machine appliqué for a casual look and a quicker process. Use thread to match the appliqué fabric if you want it to blend in, or use contrasting thread to

highlight the form. For details, such as eyes on any animals, machine-embroider them as you appliqué. On the ladybug, for example, I continued beyond the appliquéd body to machine-embroider the legs (see Tools and Techniques, page 21, for more information on appliqué).

12 Complete the appliqués for the other side of the quilt.

Finish the Quilt

13 Create your quilt sandwich. Place the day side on the bottom of your layers face down, place the batting next, and then place the night side on the top face up. Pin or baste the quilt sandwich together (see Tools and Techniques, page 22).

14 The finishing construction becomes an integral part of the design of this quilt's day-and-night theme. Use white or light-colored floss to tie the quilt. With the knots on the night side, they will appear as little stars on the dark fabric and disappear into the sky of the day side. You may even want to arrange them in astronomically accurate configurations. Alternatively, you could hand- or machine-quilt stars in white. Or do some of both! Keep track of both sides of the quilt so you don't end up with ties or quilted stars on the day side where you don't want them.

15 Bind the quilt with bias binding so it will curve around the quilt. Rejoice that there are no corners to navigate! Use purchased bias binding. Audition your binding on both the day and night sides of the quilt. You may want to use a green or brown binding to give your scene a ground line, a fun stripe that picks up colors from both sides, or whatever your settings require.

MATERIALS

* A variety of felted wool knits that equal about 7½ yd × 40" (6.9 m × 101.5 cm) or 5 yd (4.6 m) of 72" (183 cm) wide felt for snowballs

* Coordinating thread

* 20 cubic feet (0.5 cubic meter) of cotton or polyester stuffing, shredded paper, newspaper, beanbag fill, or shredded foam

* 6 off-white zippers: two 14" (35.5 cm), two 20" (51 cm), and two 24" (61 cm)

* A variety of felt for accessories

* Fabric glue or glue gun

* The hook side of scraps of adhesive Velcro for accessories (optional)

* 1–2 yd (91.5 cm–1.8 m) of 24" (61 cm) wide fusible interfacing (optional)

* 7½ yd (6.9 m) of 40"–45" (101.5-114.5 cm) wide muslin for lining (optional)

* 3 off-white zippers: 14" (35.5 cm), 18" (45.5 cm), and 24" (61 cm) for lining (optional)

TOOLS

* Basic Sewing Kit

* Indoor Snowman patterns on sides B, C, and D of the insert

* Zipper foot

FINISHED SIZE

The snowballs are about 36" (91.5 cm) in diameter, 24" (61 cm) in diameter, and 18" (45.5 cm) in diameter. They will settle on top of each other to make a 56" (142 cm) tall snowman.

Indoor Snowman

A friend, a toy, a set of giant pillows— this snowman has a sophisticated feel that makes it as perfect in your living room as it is in a play room. You can make the snowballs as large or as small as you like simply by enlarging the patterns. The Indoor Snowman is a wonderful gift for a family or a school, either completed or as a basic snowman with a pile of felt that children can use to make the features.

To make the snowballs, you can either piece together a variety of felted wools or use felt yardage. If you're using felt yardage, skip to the second part of Step 3. For felted wools, you'll puzzle the fabrics together for each pattern piece. Have fun with this. You can use old sweaters, scarves, mittens, and hats in all shades of white (see Tools and Techniques, page 19, for felting instructions).

Pure 100% wool works best, but it's not absolutely necessary. Test the fabrics in your washer and dryer.

I have had very good results with combinations of wool, angora, and small percentages of nylon or rayon. Search for blankets in thrift stores where you can get lots of material for little money. If you're piecing your snowman, you'll need extra fusible interfacing for all of your patchwork seams (see Step 2 below).

Also, you can stuff your snowman with a variety of beanbag fillings, packing peanuts, your favorite fiberfill, or even crumpled newspaper or shredded paper. Remove the paper for snowball washing or to

store it flat. The instructions include optional snowball liners, which are quick to sew and make it easier to wash the outer cover and replace the filler if needed. For the liners, you can use muslin or any leftover fabric, including old bed sheets or tablecloths.

Over time, the filling will pack down and you will need to add more; how much depends on the filling you use. I filled my Indoor Snowman with 25 pounds (11.3 kg) of recycled upholstery foam, which is sold as bean bag-chair fill.

1 Cut straight-sided pieces (rectangles, squares, strips, etc.) from your pieces of felted wool knits. Lay them out like a puzzle and add extra strips or trim pieces as needed. Test out the size by laying your Small, Medium, and Large Snowball pattern pieces over the patched fabric (**FIGURE 1**).

2 This step is optional, but if your snowman will get heavy use or be subjected to lots of silliness and excessive lounging, I recommend you reinforce the seams. Cut 1" (2.5 cm) wide strips from the fusible interfacing. Butt the edges of two felted wool pieces together and fuse the strips to the inside, covering the butt joint. This will help the seam stay together as you are sewing, as well as keep the seam strong.

3 Stitch the seams on the right side with the widest zigzag stitch. Piece together enough fabric to make seven sections for each size snowball. Use the Indoor Snowman Snowball patterns from the insert to cut out the seven sections for each size snowball.

4 Decide how the sections will be arranged around each snowball. Make sure any pockets or other details that remain from the felted sweaters are facing the way you would like them. Label each section, in order from 1 to 7, using tape or by pinning a scrap of paper to each section.

5 Reinforce the seam between sections 1 and 2 and join the seams using a wide zigzag stitch. Then reinforce and sew sections 3 and 4 together.

6 You will need to be able to unzip each snowball to almost half of its circumference in order to insert the stuffed liner. Readily available zippers will not be long enough for your snowballs, so you will need two for each. The zippers are sewn so they meet in the middle and unzip to either side.

Add the zippers between sections 5 and 6. Instead of reinforcing the seam between sections 5 and 6, baste it together with a wide and long zigzag stitch. Mark the midpoint of the seam.

7 Pin the zippers to the inside of the seam with the zipper pulls starting at the midpoint and the rest of each zipper going to each side. Make sure the zipper pull is positioned facing the wrong side of the snowball.

8 Using a zipper foot, topstitch the zippers to the snowball on the long sides. Cut the basting threads. If your zippers don't quite meet the points where all of the sections come together, butt join the remainder of the seam and zigzag stitch them together.

9 Reinforce and sew section 7 to section 1, section 2 to section 3 and section 4 to section 5. Sew section 6 to section 7. You will need to unzip the zippers and use the opening to get the fabric into the sewing machine.

10 Using the Pole Cover pattern, cut six circles from leftover scraps. Machine sew the circles over the north and south poles of each snowball with a zigzag stitch, or handsew using a blanket stitch. This will take the stress off the joint where all the points come together as well as make everything look nice and neat.

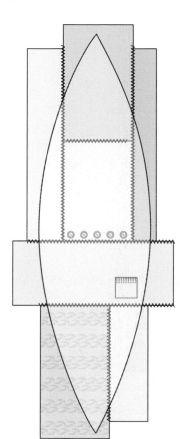

fig. 1

Test size by laying pattern piece over patched fabric.

Make the Optional Linings

11 Use the Indoor Snowman Snowball patterns and cut seven of each size from muslin. The liners use the same patterns as the snowballs, but they only have one zipper each. The liners also have a ¼" (6 mm) seam allowance, compared to the butt-joined snowballs.

12 For each snowball's lining, sew sections 1 and 2 together. Then sew sections 3 and 4 together.

13 Add the zipper between sections 5 and 6. Following the markings on the pattern, sew the seam on either side of the zipper opening with a regular straight stitch. Sew the zipper opening with a long, straight basting stitch. Start at one end with a ¼" (6 mm) seam

allowance, then gradually increase the seam allowance to ⅝" (1.5 cm) for the entire length of the zipper opening. Gradually decrease back to a ¼" (6 mm) seam allowance on the other side of the zipper opening.

14 Press the seam open. Pin the zipper to the inside of the basted opening with the zipper teeth facing the wrong side of the snowball lining. Using a zipper foot, topstitch the zipper to the snowball lining,

going around all four sides of the zipper. Remove the basting stitches.

15 Sew section 7 to section 1, section 2 to section 3, and section 4 to section 5. Sew section 6 to section 7 using the zipper opening to get the fabric into the sewing machine.

16 Because the lining is made from muslin, which has little stretch, the north and south poles

Kid Work

★ Search for white wool sweaters, hats, and mittens
★ Sew the lining and piece the snowballs
★ Stuff the snowballs
★ Create drawings for features
★ Make snowman features

where all seven points come together will be under stress. To reinforce them, cut out six circles about 4½" (11.5 cm) in diameter from leftover felt or felted wool. Sew a circle on each snowball's poles.

Finish the Snowballs

17 Stuff your snowball linings, dividing the fill between them so all three snowballs are the same firmness. Then insert the stuffed lining into the appropriate size snowball cover.

Make the Snowman Features

18 Set your kids loose with scissors and a pile of felt. For multilayered features, give them fabric glue or a glue gun.

19 Smaller pieces of felt will stick to your snowman on their own, but larger and multi-layered pieces may need some help from the Velcro. Use the hook side of adhesive Velcro cut into suitable lengths.

MATERIALS

For the quilt:

* 3½ yd (3.2 m) of a variety of felted wool wovens and knits, quilting fabric scraps, flannel, velvet, plush, corduroy, and fleece

* 4½ yd (4.1 m) cotton fabric or flannel for quilt backing

* 58" × 84" (147.5 × 213 cm) batting

* ¾ yd (68.5 cm) flannel or cotton for quilt binding

* Coordinating thread

* Contrasting thread

* Variety of buttons for landscape elements

* Embroidery floss for grass tufts and hand-quilting

For the movable elements:
(These are all suggestions and optional supplies, depending on the elements you add.)

* Scraps of felt or felted wool, netting, and extra heavy interfacing

* Cotton or polyester fill

* Trims such as rickrack, ball fringe, bias tape, and ruffles

* Felt balls and buttons

* ⅛"–½" (2 mm–1.3 cm) wide ribbons

* Beads

* Embroidery floss

TOOLS

* Basic Sewing Kit

* Over in the Meadow Landscape Rug patterns on sides B and D of the insert

- -

continued on next page ☞

Over in the Meadow Landscape Rug

The Landscape Rug is really a fabulous quilt with separate elements for playing. Depending on your color palette, your Landscape Rug may be realistic or entirely fantastic. Use an array of warm greens and browns with yellows and oranges mixed in for realism or use candy colors for a fairy world. Focus on one element at a time, and you will be surprised at how quickly you have a magical land. Take small swatches with you on your search for other materials. The materials hunt is half the fun. Texture is what makes this project so fabulous and so fun to make and play with Be sure to include a variety of wonderfully touchable textures.

* Walking foot
* Pinking shears (optional)
* ¼" (6 mm) hole/circle punch (optional)

FINISHED SIZE
This quilt shown is 54" × 80" (137 × 203 cm), but you can make yours smaller. Consider a 12" × 18" (30.5 × 45.5 cm) travel mat.

You can make the full quilt or just a mini play mat. Add a small hill, a shrub or two, and some rocks and flowers—a lovely little world! Collect materials, stitch together the ground quilt, and make the movable elements. This project is an exercise in sharpening your own creativity. Don't be afraid to improvise and make your quilt blocks askew. I like to make this quilt by laying things out, stitching as I go, and then squaring up the edges at the end.

I encourage you to play, experiment, and make this quilt your very own. Do a quick sketch on graph paper with some colored pencils. Get your children to join you and see what they come up with. Your landscape can always change as you go.

If you are more of an intuitive maker and like to improvise, go ahead and start cutting. Squares and rectangles of different sizes are a good place to start. Then you can arrange them like a puzzle. If you end up a bit short on one element, just add another strip. Think organically, just like a landscape. Make some areas with many smaller pieces and some big open areas.

Make the Rug

1 First, design your quilt top. Collect your various fabrics and wash them all beforehand to make sure they will hold up.

Lay out your quilt like a puzzle. Start with the different types of ground you know you want to include, such as grass or a large field. Then fill in around those patches. If you don't want to improvise, follow the layout chart for my Landscape Rug **(FIGURE 1)**.

2 Piece your patches together. The key to stitching together this type of puzzle is to avoid sewing into corners. Think of the quilt as a series of smaller quilts: work in sections and then sew them together. If you're making a smaller quilt, sew up just a section or two at a time, using **FIGURE 2** on page 72 as a guide for construction.

If you are having trouble sewing bulky, textured blocks such as chenille or knit, switch in a matching-size block of cotton or flannel, then appliqué the bulky block on top.

3 Pin the quilt top to the batting and backing (see Tools and Techniques, page 22, for tips) so you can quilt the rug.

I like to use a variety of quilting techniques. I used "valley stitching" to stabilize the heavier fabrics, and the stitching practically disappeared into the texture. Straight lines of machine quilting add subtle texture while highlighting the grid quality of the quilt.

Try tying the quilt with floss and yarn for instant grass and plants; tie randomly or create an orderly grid. Hand-quilting with floss and larger stitches is also very fitting. Use several techniques to highlight various

sections of your quilt. **FIGURE 3** on page 74 shows the types of quilting I used on my Landscape Rug.

Use wood or shell buttons as rocks, which will also help hold the quilt together. Tie the buttons to your landscape with the floss knots on the front or back.

4 Bind the quilt. I used flannel cut into 3" (7.5 cm) wide strips. Now get ready to have lots of fun making the movable stuff!

Stitch the Movable Elements

When you make the individual elements, experiment with your favorite materials. Trees, mountains, and other landscape elements are perfect for using all those fabulous trims and buttons you have been eyeing. Many of the elements are not based on patterns, so cut whatever lovely circles, ovals, and organic shapes your scissors desire. All materials are scraps smaller than 12" (30.5 cm) square unless otherwise indicated.

MAKE A POND

A pond is a simple way to make a high-impact element (see photo on page 73). Make a large lake, a simple pond, or a river—just cut the pieces into different sizes and shapes. Try adding an island in the middle with the techniques for making a hill.

5 Cut a large, organic pond shape from your felt or felted wool. No pattern here, just use your scissors! Then cut a smaller shape from a different color.

Sew the smaller shape to the larger shape by hand using a backstitch and contrasting floss. I used metallic floss, which can be hard to work with, but I couldn't resist it for a

fig. 1

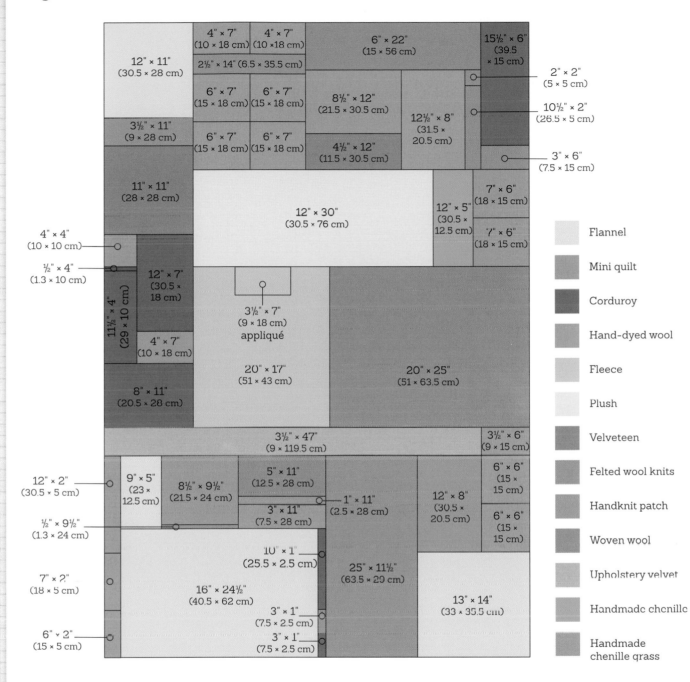

12" × 11" (30.5 × 28 cm)

4" × 7" (10 × 18 cm)

4" × 7" (10 ×18 cm)

2½" × 14" (6.5 × 35.5 cm)

6" × 22" (15 × 56 cm)

15½" × 6" (39.5 × 15 cm)

6" × 7" (15 × 18 cm)

6" × 7" (15 × 18 cm)

8½" × 12" (21.5 × 30.5 cm)

12½" × 8" (31.5 × 20.5 cm)

2" × 2" (5 × 5 cm)

10½" × 2" (26.5 × 5 cm)

3½" × 11" (9 × 28 cm)

6" × 7" (15 × 18 cm)

6" × 7" (15 × 18 cm)

4½" × 12" (11.5 × 30.5 cm)

3" × 6" (7.5 × 15 cm)

11" × 11" (28 × 28 cm)

12" × 30" (30.5 × 76 cm)

12" × 5" (30.5 × 12.5 cm)

7" × 6" (18 × 15 cm)

7" × 6" (18 × 15 cm)

4" × 4" (10 × 10 cm)

½" × 4" (1.3 × 10 cm)

11½" × 4" (29 × 10 cm)

12" × 7" (30.5 × 18 cm)

3½" × 7" (9 × 18 cm) appliqué

20" × 17" (51 × 43 cm)

20" × 25" (51 × 63.5 cm)

4" × 7" (10 × 18 cm)

8" × 11" (20.5 × 28 cm)

3½" × 47" (9 × 119.5 cm)

3½" × 6" (9 × 15 cm)

12" × 2" (30.5 × 5 cm)

9" × 5" (23 × 12.5 cm)

8½" × 9½" (21.5 × 24 cm)

5" × 11" (12.5 × 28 cm)

6" × 6" (15 × 15 cm)

½" × 9½" (1.3 × 24 cm)

3" × 11" (7.5 × 28 cm)

1" × 11" (2.5 × 28 cm)

12" × 8" (30.5 × 20.5 cm)

6" × 6" (15 × 15 cm)

10" × 1" (25.5 × 2.5 cm)

7" × 2" (18 × 5 cm)

16" × 24½" (40.5 × 62 cm)

25" × 11½" (63.5 × 29 cm)

13" × 14" (33 × 35.5 cm)

3" × 1" (7.5 × 2.5 cm)

6" × 2" (15 × 5 cm)

3" × 1" (7.5 × 2.5 cm)

Flannel

Mini quilt

Corduroy

Hand-dyed wool

Fleece

Plush

Velveteen

Felted wool knits

Handknit patch

Woven wool

Upholstery velvet

Handmade chenille

Handmade chenille grass

fig. 2

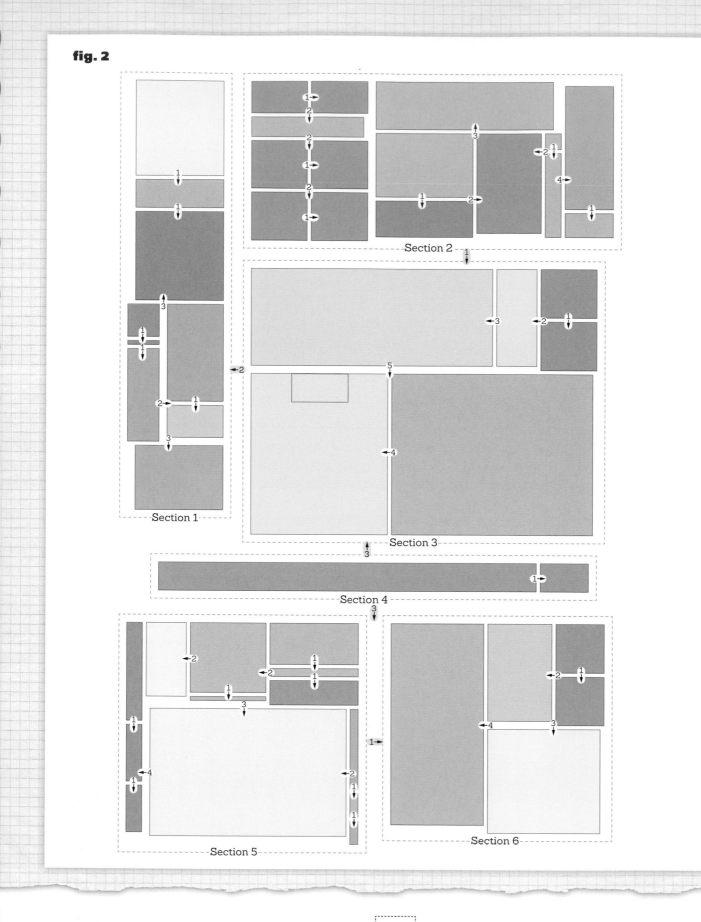

Section 1

Section 2

Section 3

Section 4

Section 5

Section 6

bit of sparkle in the pond. Work in an uneven spiral from the outside toward the middle.

Cut a piece of interfacing ⅛" (3 mm) smaller than the pond all the way around. Place the interfacing on a larger piece of felt, which becomes the base. Then stack the pond on top. Topstitch the pond onto the base all around the edge. Trim the base even with the top or use pinking shears to make a decorative edge.

MAKE TREES

All of the trees need a base in order to stand up. You can make a single tree with a base or a stand of trees on one base. Make sure your trees are not too heavy on top and that the bottom of the trunk is wide enough to hold up the tree. The larger you make the base, the more stable it will be. Experiment with your own trees or try the ones described here.

6 The **Branched Tree** also requires small amounts of netting or tulle for the top.

For each tree, cut two or three felt rectangles for the trunks 2–3" (5–7.5 cm) wide and 2½–4" (6.5–10 cm) high. Fold the shapes in half lengthwise and machine sew them together along the long edge with a ⅛" (3 mm) seam allowance.

Leave the seams on the outside and sew the trunks together to form branches, or leave them separate. Stuff the trunks and branches.

Cut rough circles from netting about 7–8" (18–20.5 cm) in diameter. Make a running stitch by hand around the edge of each net circle. Pull in the thread to gather the edges and make a puff. Secure with a few stitches.

Insert the gathered end of the net circle into the end of the trunk or branch. Sew the netting in securely.

7 The **Tropical Tree** also requires scraps of cotton fabric and bits of batting for leaves.

Using the Tropical Tree Trunk pattern, cut out the trunk, fold in half lengthwise with right side out, and handsew the long side closed.

Cut out the leaves from fabric and batting, following the Tropical Tree Leaf patterns. Match fabric with right sides together and place on top of the batting. Sew around the curved edge of the leaves; the straight edge remains open.

Clip the curves and turn, with right sides of fabric out and batting on the inside. Press.

8 Hand- or machine-quilt the leaves. Working with the raw open edge, fold a leaf and tack with two or three stitches to hold in place.

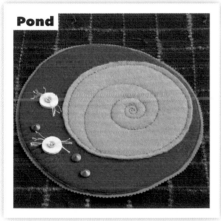

Pond

Branched Tree

Tropical Tree

Stacked Tree

Lollipop Tree

fig. 3

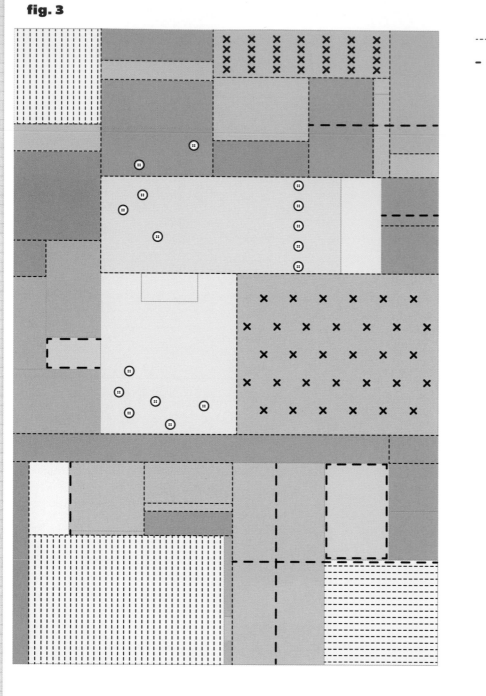

----------	Machine quilted
— — —	Hand quilted with floss
✗	Tied with floss
⊕	Buttons

Working your way around (as if adding petals to a rose), keep adding leaves and tacking them in place.

9 Insert the raw edge of the leaf roll into the top of the trunk. Sew firmly in place. Stuff the trunk from the bottom.

10 The **Stacked Tree** (see photo on page 73) also requires felt circles or felt buttons for the top layers.

Cut the trunk 4½" (11.5 cm) wide and as tall as you would like your tree to be (probably 2½–4" (6.5–10 cm). Fold in half lengthwise, right side out, and sew the long side closed by hand. Stuff the trunk.

11 Cut circles from thick felt or wool, 1–3½" (2.5–9 cm) in diameter. Stack the circles with the largest on the bottom. Using floss, sew by hand up from the bottom through each layer to the top and then sew back down to the bottom. Sew the tree top to the trunk.

12 The **Lollipop Tree** (see photo on page 73) also

requires scraps of cotton fabric for the treetop and perhaps some miniature buttons.

For the trunk, cut two strips of felt in one color (A) and three strips in a contrasting color (B) 4¾" × 1½" (12 × 3.8 cm). Use pinking shears to trim one long edge on both A strips and two B strips.

To form the trunk, start with the remaining unpinked B strip with two smooth long edges. Layer an A strip on top of the unpinked B strip ½" (1.3 cm) up from the bottom of the B strip. Turn the trunk over and sew along the top edge of the B strip. Add another B strip ½" (1.3 cm) up from the bottom of the A strip and sew along the top edge. Add the final A strip the same way.

Handsew the final B strip in place from the back, going through the felt only part of the way so the stitches do not show on the front. Fold the trunk in half lengthwise with wrong sides together and sew the long sides together. Stuff the trunk.

13 Using the Lollipop Tree Top pattern, cut six pieces from the cotton fabric. Place two sections with right sides together, and sew together along one long side. Continue to add sections onto the treetop until all of the sections are connected.

Bring around the last two raw edges to meet, right sides together. Sew together, leaving an opening about 1½" (3.8 cm) long in the middle of the seam.

Clip the curves and turn the treetop right side out. Stuff the treetop and sew the opening closed. This is a squat globe, not perfectly round. Sew the treetop onto the trunk and add mini buttons for fruit if desired.

MAKE TREE BASES

The size of each base depends on which trees you're grouping together and how many are in your group. Trees with heavier tops need bigger bases to balance out the weight.

14 Cut an organic shape such as a rough circle or an oval from interfacing. My bases range from 3½" × 4½" (9 × 11.5 cm) to 7" × 9" (18 × 23 cm). Place the interfacing on top of a bigger piece of felt. Cut the felt out ⅛" (3 mm) larger than the interfacing all around.

 chapter 2: play

Layered Hill

Pieced Hill

Mountain/Conical tree

Switch the felt with the interfacing, then place both on top of another bigger piece of felt, sandwiching the interfacing between the felt. Cut a matching piece of felt for the bottom or cut the bottom bigger than the top and use pinking shears to create a decorative edge around the bottom. Topstitch the top of the base to the bottom of the base.

15 Handsew the trees to the base. Add bushes, flowers, and button rocks as desired.

MAKE HILLS

Hills can be a simple addition to your landscape or a crazy, major element. Their basic shape is perfect for embellishment, and they can be used as a base for trees, flowers, and rocks. Don't overstuff them, or your hill or mountain won't sit flat.

16 The **Layered Hill** is made by layering the fabric and then stuffing the layers. Use fabrics with some stretch so the layers will puff up nicely and you can ease the edges in smoothly.

Cut a series of circles and ovals of different sizes. The shapes for the hills in my Landscape Rug range from 1¾–8" (4.5–20.5 cm).

Place the smallest hill on top of the second smallest hill. Working your way around the hill, scooch the edges toward the center about ¼–½" (6 mm–1.3 cm), and pin. This will ease in the circumference so the center will puff up. Topstitch the hill onto the one beneath it.

From the back, cut a small slit in the underside of the hill. Stuff.

Continue to add increasingly larger hills underneath. You can add trims in between the layers. Trim the bottom about ½" (1.3 cm) from the edge of the largest hill.

17 Make the base. Cut a piece of interfacing ⅛" (3 mm) smaller than the bottom all the way around. Place the interfacing on a larger piece of felt and then place the hill on top. Topstitch the hill onto the base all around the edge.

Trim the base even with the top. Use pinking shears to make a decorative edge or cut the interfacing and base even with the bottom of the hill.

18 The **Pieced Hill** is made by piecing sections together to form a dome. Add ribbon loops on top for a whimsical touch.

Cut six sections from the Pieced Hill pattern. With right sides together, sew sections together to create a dome shape, stopping the stitches ¼" (6 mm) from the top of the dome. Turn right side out.

19 Cut random lengths of ribbon about 3–4" (7.5–10 cm) long, then loop and sew the raw edges together. Insert these loops into the top of dome and tack in place from the inside with a few stitches. Stuff the hill.

20 Using the pattern, cut one Base from felt and one from interfacing. Topstitch the base and interfacing together ⅛" (3 mm) from the edge. Trim the interfacing close to the stitching. Handsew the base onto the hill.

MAKE MOUNTAINS OR CONICAL TREES

These simple cones become mountains, trees, or even little houses depending on what size and color they are and what trims you add. You'll also need pieces of felt ranging in size from an 18" (45.5 cm) square or 13" × 24" (33 × 61 cm) rectangle for the largest mountain top and a 12" (30.5 cm) square for the largest mountain base.

Garden

Shrubs

Topiaries

21 Cut a mountain from felt using the Small Mountain, Medium Mountain, or Large Mountain pattern. To make a tree, cut one from felt using the Small Conical Tree, Medium Conical Tree, or Large Conical Tree pattern. Overlap the two straight edges slightly and stitch closed by hand.

If adding trim, sew it along the curved bottom edge or stitch it in a spiral from the top to the bottom. Stuff the cone.

22 Using the pattern from the insert, cut one corresponding Mountain or Conical Tree Base from felt and one from interfacing, then topstitch them together ⅛" (3 mm) from the edge. Trim the interfacing close to the stitching.

Handsew the base onto the mountain. Add a felt ball to the top if desired.

MAKE A GARDEN

The concept of a garden can be interpreted in many ways. A tidy grid is reminiscent of a vegetable patch. Or try a tangle of wildflowers—all you need is some felt, a hole punch, ribbon scraps, and a few beads to make flower magic.

23 Cut a piece of wool 6" × 6½" (15 × 16.5 cm). Sew rows of felt balls on by hand. Then, sew on buttons using floss in contrasting colors. Baste rickrack or other trims underneath the outer edge of the garden.

24 Cut a piece of interfacing 5" × 5¾" (12.5 × 14.5 cm). Sandwich the interfacing between the garden and the larger piece of felt for the base, then topstitch the garden onto the base. Trim the base to just beyond the rickrack.

MAKE FLOWERS

(Flowers shown on top of the Layered Hill.) You can use a tiny circle punch to add holes around the edges of the flowers for a lacy effect. Sprinkle the flowers throughout the landscape.

25 Cut circles about ⅝–⅞" (1.5–2.2 cm) in diameter from felt. Use a ¼" (6 mm) hole punch to make felt circles in contrasting colors for the centers. For a more organic shape, cut out centers with scissors.

26 Insert the needle from the bottom of the flower. Using contrasting thread, sew the center onto the flower.

Start on one edge of the center and make a stitch directly across the center and down through the flower at the other edge. Come back up at the center's edge about ⅛" (3 mm) from where you went in and continue to make stitches across the center circle, forming a star. When you have worked your way around the circle, come up through the center and tie a French knot (see Tools and Techniques, page 20) or go through a bead. Go back down through the flower layers and secure the thread on the back of the flower.

27 To add stems, cut ⅛" (3 mm) ribbon into lengths 1–2" (2.5–5 cm) long. Place two lengths of ribbon on top of each other and sew down the center lengthwise. Cut a ⅝–⅞" (1.5–2.2 cm) circle, and punch holes around edge. Punch a hole in the center with the ¹⁄₁₆" (2 mm) punch or use a sharp scissors point to make a hole.

Insert the stem into the center hole so that ⅛" (3 mm) of the stem sticks out the top. Separate the top of the two stem ribbons and splay them down against the felt circle. Sew the flower center and bead on top of the splayed ribbon stem, tucking the stems in so they are hidden by the flower center.

Cultivate a Landscape

I made a few special patches within my Landscape Rug. These include a wild meadow knitted from highly textured yarn, two types of chenille patches, and a mini quilt that suggests a garden. Try some of these, or experiment with your own.

Fuzzy chenille patch

MATERIALS

* Scraps of cotton fabric for patch-work-garden mini quilt
* 1 yd (91.5 cm) total of flannel fabrics
* Coordinating thread
* Contrasting thread

TOOLS

* Basic Sewing Kit
* Walking foot

Make a Patchwork Garden

① These special patches are like mini quilts! Sew scraps of quilting fabric into rows. Trim the edges straight and sew the rows together to create a block **(FIGURE 1)**.

Make a Fuzzy Chenille Patch

① Decide how big to make the patch and cut four layers of flannel to that size on the bias. The chenille patch in my landscape rug is 5" × 12" (12.5 × 30.5 cm). Cut a base piece of flannel 1" (2.5 cm) larger than your flannel layers on all sides, then stack the four layers on top.

② Sew down the width of the stack ⅜" (1 cm) from the end of the stack. Continue sewing parallel rows ⅝" (1.5 cm) apart until you get to the end of the stack.

③ Cut the top four layers in between the rows of stitching, leaving the base whole.

④ To make the block fluffy, machine-wash and dry it before sewing it to the quilt top.

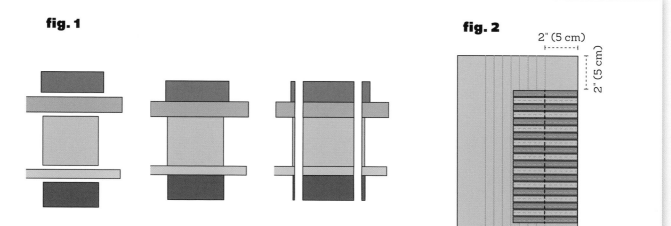

fig. 1

fig. 2

2" (5 cm)

2" (5 cm)

Make Chenille Grass

① If you make a chenille grass area with a base of 4" × 7" (10 × 18 cm), the grass will flop over the edges and appear to be 7" × 10" (18 × 25.5 cm). Cut four strips of flannel on the bias 6" × 40" (15 × 101.5 cm).

② Layer the four fabrics directly on top of each other and pin them together. Sew down the length of the flannel a scant ¼" (6 mm) from one edge. Continue to sew lines of stitching down the length, working each row ⅜" (1 cm) away from the previous row.

③ Cut the flannel stack widthwise into 4" (10 cm) sections. Cut the sections into 160 strips by cutting halfway between each row of stitching. Cut a piece of flannel for the base 7½" × 12" (19 × 30.5 cm). You will trim this down later.

④ Starting 2" (5 cm) in from one long side of the base flannel, mark eight lines down the length of the flannel ½" (1.3 cm) apart. Center one strip perpendicular to the first line and 2" (5 cm) from the top edge **(FIGURE 2)**. Pin 19 more flannel strips down the same line.

⑤ Sew down the middle of the strips along the marked line, and then flip them away from the next marked line. Center 20 more flannel strips perpendicularly down the next marked line and sew. Repeat for all eight marked lines and 160 strips.

⑥ To finish, machine-wash and dry. Trim the base fabric to 4½" × 7½" (11.5 × 18 cm).

28 To attach the flower to the landscape, make a hole in the ground material. Insert the bottom of the stem about ½" (1.3 cm) and splay the ribbon on the back side of the ground. Tack in place **(FIGURE 4)**.

MAKE SHRUBS AND BUSHES

29 **Polka Dot Bushes** (see photo on page 77) can be a great way to get your kids involved in this project by having them make the felt balls (see page 24).

Choose one side of a large felt ball as the bottom of the bush and tie a securing knot there with contrasting floss. Bring the needle out randomly all over the ball, making French knots as you go. Finish with a few securing stitches on the bottom.

Cut a circle of felt to cover the bottom and handsew it into place.

30 **Topiaries** (see photo on page 77) can be stacked by even very young children.

Stack felt balls and circles, alternating one on top of the other, with a circle on the bottom and a ball on the top. Starting from the bottom and using embroidery floss, bring your needle through the bottom circle and leave about 3" (7.5 cm) of floss hanging. Go up through the balls and circles until you are through the element second from the top. Insert the needle into the top ball and then out again ¼–½" (6 mm–1.3 cm) away, depending on the size of the ball.

Go back down through all of the other elements until you are at the bottom again, coming out ¼" (6 mm) from where you went in. Tie the two ends together.

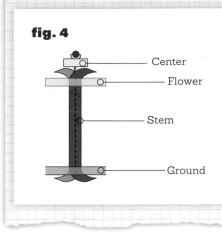

fig. 4

Center
Flower
Stem
Ground

31 **Ribbon Bushes** (shown with the Stacked Tree on page 73) can be sewn onto a tree base or anywhere in a garden block or on a hill.

Cut lengths of ribbon about 3" (7.5 cm) long, making some slightly shorter and some slightly longer. Fold the ribbons in half widthwise with cut ends matching.

Choose one ribbon and make a stitch or two about ¼" (6 mm) from the cut ends. Choose a second ribbon and sew it near the first ribbon with a few stitches. This is the center of the bush. Continue to add ribbons around the center, sewing as you go. You will have a bush with loops on the top and roots made from the cut ends.

32 To make the base of the bush, cut a circle of felt about 1" (2.5 cm) in diameter and cut a small hole in the center. Insert the root end of the bush into the hole and sew around the felt hole, attaching the bush to the felt.

Splay the roots and trim any ribbons that stick out beyond the felt circle.

chapter 3:
celebrate

No matter how small or simple, celebrations are wonderful to share with your children. Beyond the daily schlepping and the teeth brushing, the insistent "what's for dinner?" and the incessant laundry, these occasions are the whipped cream on hot chocolate.

Because you are a maker, you can increase the fun of every festivity by making special things for each celebration. The process will someday elicit those "remember whens" as much as the actual occasion. This here is exponential joy!

The projects in this chapter emphasize the importance of coming together. The Community Quilt (page 92) can be made over and over with different groups of children, and it will be different every time. You will never forget the excitement on the little makers' faces as they present their gift to a favorite teacher or a cherished grandparent. The Party Anytime Garland and Chandelier (page 82) create a tangible memory of a special occasion. Make them before the event with your child, decorate with them during the party, and hang them in your child's bedroom when the guests have gone home.

The Happy Birthday Quilt (page 86) uses your kids' drawings and writings to craft a guaranteed family treasure. The Official Flower Dance Academy Umbrella (page 100) will foster magical parties as well as Broadway-worthy performances right from your couch; there will be tickets to make, refreshments for intermission, and standing ovations for sure.

MATERIALS

* 11 yd (10 m) of ⅛" (3 mm) ribbon for garland base

* 300 pieces of a variety of materials for garland embellishments, such as ribbons, sequins, felt shapes, rectangles, feathers, pom-poms, and bells

* Coordinating or contrasting thread

* 2¼ yd (2 m) of ¼" (6 mm) boning with ⅝" (1.5 cm) fabric covering for chandelier

* 12½ yd (11.4 m) of ⅜" (1 cm) wide ribbon for chandelier

* Sixteen ½" (1.3 cm) assorted or matching buttons

* ¼–1 yd (23–91.5 cm) tulle for garland (optional)

* Fabric paint (optional)

TOOLS

* Basic Sewing Kit

* Binder clip (optional)

* Paintbrush (optional)

FINISHED SIZE

The garland is 11 yd (10 m) long. The chandelier is 52" × 18" × 18" (132 × 45.5 × 45.5 cm) from the bottom to the top hanging knot.

Party Anytime Garland and Chandelier

Festive and whimsical, a garland just says celebration. But then what do you do with the garland after the party has ended? You can turn it into a decorative chandelier! Having a party to welcome a new baby? Use the garland for the party and then complete the chandelier frame with it and hang it over the baby's crib or changing table. A special birthday? Afterward, turn the garland into a chandelier for the child's bedroom as a memento. The garland loops over buttons on the chandelier frame so it can be removed easily and used again as a garland. Give the chandelier a new look by making a different garland and looping it over the buttons.

You can make the garland any length you like to fit your celebration, but you will need a 10⅔ yd (9.8 m) garland to assemble the chandelier. You'll divide the garland in half: one 5⅓ yd (4.9 m) piece for the top ring and one 5⅓ yd (4.9 m) piece for the bottom ring of the chandelier. About 300 pieces of embellishment will yield a garland of the same density as mine, as long as you sew on an element every 1½–2" (3.8–5 cm). Of course, you can make your garland sparser or denser.

1 Assemble the elements. Cut the ribbon into 2–6" (5–15 cm) sections, the tulle into 4" × 8" (10 × 20.5 cm) pieces, and the felt into a variety of shapes.

2 Sew the garland. Starting several inches from one end of the ribbon, sew down the center of the ribbon and over the elements, adding them as you go. For the tulle, scrunch the tulle by hand down the lengthwise center and then sew it through the scrunched part onto the ribbon. Sew all the way to the end of the ribbon.

If you need to piece the ribbon, overlap the end of the new ribbon with the previous ribbon and continue stitching down the center, joining them. You can also sew the elements to each ribbon section separately, leaving 4" (10 cm) or so on each end of the ribbons to tie them together.

3 If you plan to use bells, stitch down a length of ⅛" (3 mm) wide ribbon wherever you want a bell. Tie the bell onto the ribbon after the sewing is complete.

Make the Chandelier Frame

4 Cut the boning into two pieces, one 53" (134.5 cm) long and one 28" (71 cm) long. Pull back the fabric covering for several inches on each end of the 53" (134.5 cm) piece. Overlap the ends about 1½" (3.8 cm) to make a circle. Using a zigzag stitch on the widest setting, zigzag the two ends together lengthwise. The needle will clear the boning on each side, wrapping the two ends together. Try using a binder clip to hold the boning together; this lets you keep your fingers out of the way while stitching the ends together.

5 Pull the fabric covering back over each end. Tuck under the raw edges so they butt together, trimming the fabric as needed. Sew the fabric ends together.

6 To coordinate your chandelier frame with your garland, paint the fabric covering on the boning rings with fabric paint.

Repeat the previous steps with the 28" (71 cm) piece. You will now have one larger ring that is about 50" (127 cm) in circumference and one smaller ring that is about 25" (63.5 cm) in circumference.

7 Mark each ring equidistantly in eight places on the outer flat surface of the ring. On the 50" (127 cm) ring, the marks will be about 6¼" (16 cm) apart. On the 25" (63.5) ring, the marks will be about 3⅛" (8 cm) apart.

8 Cut eight 55" (139.5 cm) lengths of the ⅜" (1 cm) ribbon.

Sew one end of one ribbon to one of the eight marked places on the small ring. Repeat with the remaining seven ribbons and seven other marked spots on the small ring. You now have eight ribbons hanging from the small ring; the next step is to attach them to the large ring.

9 Mark each ribbon 12" (30.5 cm) from the spot where it is attached to the small ring. Sew the marked place on one ribbon to one of the marked places on the large ring.

Repeat with the remaining seven ribbons and seven other marked spots on the large ring. The two rings are now attached with 12" (30.5 cm) of each of the eight ribbons between them.

10 Mark each ribbon 16" (40.5 cm) from the place where it is attached to the large ring. Gather the ribbons together at the marks. Knot the ribbons in a single overhand knot, making sure the marks are not visible at the base of the knot. Using all of the ribbons, tie another knot 16" (40.5 cm) from the first knot. This is the top of the chandelier and will be used for hanging.

Sew one button at each of the eight points on the small ring and the eight points on the large ring where the ribbons are sewn to the boning. The buttons will be used to loop the garland onto the chandelier.

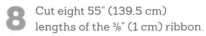

Kid Work

★ Choose colors and materials
★ Measure and mark the ribbons for the garland
★ Paint the boning rings
★ Cut ribbon sections and felt shapes
★ Hand materials to the sewist

Assemble the Chandelier

11 Cut the garland in half. You should have two pieces each about 5⅓ yd (4.9 m) long. Mark each piece into eight sections of about 24" (61 cm). You can mark some sections a bit smaller and some a bit larger to make it more interesting.

12 Loop the garland onto the buttons on the large ring, looping each marked spot on the garland with a button on the ring. This will create the garland's swags. Repeat with the remaining garland and the small ring.

How you hang the chandelier will depend on your ceilings. A simple nail, screw, or hook through the center of the top ribbon knot should be sufficient. Be sure that whatever you choose is appropriate for your ceiling material and will support the weight, however light, of the chandelier, especially if you are hanging it over a crib or changing table.

MATERIALS

* 1¼ yd (1.1 m) of cotton fabric for quilt top

* 1¼ yd (1.1 m) of cotton fabric for quilt backing

* Cotton fabric scraps for appliqué

* Cotton fabric scraps for petal edging

* ½ yd (45.5 cm) of cotton fabric for binding

* Coordinating thread

* Contrasting thread

* Embroidery floss

* 46" (117 cm) square of batting

TOOLS

* Basic Sewing Kit

* The Happy Birthday Quilt Petal patterns on side A of the insert

* Child's drawings and writings

FINISHED SIZE

The Happy Birthday Quilt oriented on point is 60" × 60" (152.5 × 152.5 cm). A square quilt will be about 41" × 41" (104 × 104 cm), plus the petal edging.

The Happy Birthday Quilt

When I was growing up, we had homemade birthday parties in our house, and now I do the same with my girls. Making things with your children is a sweet way to create more memories around family traditions. Your kids will remember the fun of making the accessories as much as the actual event. The Happy Birthday Quilt is a great addition to whatever birthday fun you already create in your family. Embroider "Happy Birthday" or another festive greeting in your children's writing and appliqué their drawings of cakes or balloons.

Use this quilt as a bed topper for whoever is having a birthday that week. At a party, use it on the present table or for the birthday child (or adult!) to sit on during an activity. Keep it out year-round as a play mat, or keep the quilt as a special treat, tucked in the closet only to emerge on a birthday. Imagine your child waking up to the Birthday Quilt as an annual birthday treat!

The size of this quilt is based on the width of standard quilter's cotton, which usually ranges from 40" to 45" (101.5–114.5 cm). Because your fabrics may be slightly different widths, these instructions show you how to cut your fabric according to the widths you have.

Your backing should be larger than your front fabric by at least 2" (5 cm) all around. The petal binding is constructed differently than a regular binding. Feel free to follow the regular binding instructions (page 23) if you prefer.

1 First, measure the width of your backing fabric from selvedge to selvedge. That number will now be referred to as X. Subtract 4" (10 cm) from X. That number will now be referred to as Y.

2 Fold the quilt-top fabric in half lengthwise with selvedges matching and square up one end. Measure Y from the squared-off end and cut the fabric to that length. Unfold the fabric and refold it in the opposite direction, so the cut edges match and the selvedges are at each end. Trim ½" (1.3 cm) off one selvedge edge. Measure Y from that cut edge and cut the fabric to that length.

3 Cut the batting into a square that is equal to the size of the quilt top.

4 Now for the fun part. Search your children's drawings and writings for the images you would like to use. Or, if you have a particular theme in mind, have your kids get started with paper and markers.

You can ask them to write out "Happy Birthday" in one go, but I like to use individual letters from different kids and arrange them ransom-note style. Use some fatter, puffy letters

to appliqué and some thin letters to embroider. Plan for some letters to have shapes of other fabrics behind them for added interest.

Also assemble drawings for your quilt's appliqués. Choose images that relate to the birthday theme or to family favorites. For my quilt, I used a birthday cake my daughter drew on a card for her father's birthday.

5 Enlarge or reduce the letters and drawings until they're the right size for your quilt. Lay them out

on the quilt-top fabric, resizing the letters and drawings as needed until you are happy with the composition. You can orient the quilt top as a straight-on square or on point.

6 Transfer the letters and drawings either directly on the quilt to embroider or on scraps of fabric to appliqué onto the quilt. Embroider and appliqué the lettering and images. (See Tools and Techniques, page 20, for more information on embroidery and appliqué.)

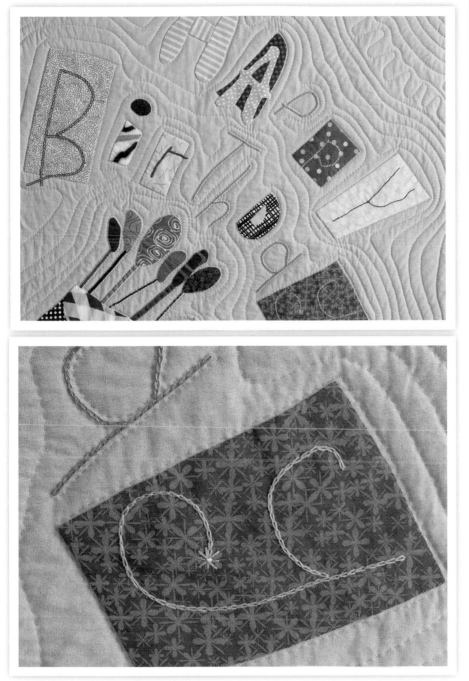

Kid Work

★ Write and draw letters and appliqué images

★ Choose fabrics and colors

★ Make petals for the binding

★ Help tie the quilt

quilting. You can tie (get the kids to help!), hand-quilt, or machine-quilt the Happy Birthday Quilt. For mine, I decided to jump in and hand-quilt. It's small enough so you can try hand-quilting without being too overwhelmed. Trim the backing and batting flush with the front fabric.

Make the
Petal Edging

I like to make each petal different, cutting them all without a pattern. You can use the Petal patterns provided in the insert or make your own petal shapes. Depending on your final quilt measurement (remember your Y measurement!), you will need about fifty to sixty petals to go around all four sides of the quilt.

8 Assemble sets of two scraps. The fabrics don't have to match, but they should coordinate. With right sides together, cut out petal shapes.

Sew around the curved part of each petal, leaving the straight edge open. Clip around the curve of each petal and turn them right side out, smoothing the curve from the inside. Press the petals.

7 Now, finish the Happy Birthday Quilt. Remember that X measurement? That is the width of your backing fabric and you will use it to cut the backing into a square. Fold the backing fabric in half lengthwise with selvedges matching and square up one end. Measure X from the squared-off end and cut the fabric to that length.

Layer the quilt backing, batting, and top and pin the sandwich throughout the entire quilt to get it ready for

least ½" (1.3 cm) on either end of the side has no petals.

13 Sew the first binding strip onto the quilt with a ½" (1.3 cm) seam allowance. Fold it over the quilt edge, tucking the ¼" (6 mm) fold with the petal seam allowance against the front of the quilt. On the back of the quilt, fold the binding under ½" (1.3 cm) and handstitch the binding in place. Cut the excess binding at the ends flush with the quilt.

Attach the second binding strip to a side of the quilt adjacent to the first binding strip. Repeat the same steps as above until you are ready to handsew the binding on the back of the quilt. Now, you can line the petals up to the end of the quilt on the corner that already has the binding.

14 Trim the end of the binding that overlaps the first binding strip ½" (1.3 cm) beyond the quilt. Tuck that ½" (1.3 cm) in to make a squared-off corner and handsew the binding in place. Trim the binding flush on the opposite end.

15 Attach the third binding strip in the same way as the second.

Attach the last binding strip in the same way as the second and third, but trim both ends of the binding strip ½" (1.3 cm) beyond the edge of the quilt and tuck both ends in. Handstitch the binding in place.

16 As always, a label is a nice touch for a quilt (see Tools and Techniques, page 25). For the Happy Birthday Quilt, create one with the names of everyone in your family and the date you made the quilt.

Make the Quilt Binding

9 You will need four separate strips of binding. Measure the binding fabric from selvedge to selvedge. If that measurement is at least 2" (5 cm) longer than your Y measurement, cut four strips of the binding fabric 2½" (6.5 cm) wide from selvedge to selvedge. If the selvedge-to-selvedge measurement is shorter than your Y measurement, cut five strips of the binding fabric 2½" (6.5 cm) wide from selvedge to selvedge. Cut one strip widthwise into four sections.

10 With short ends matching and right sides together, sew one short piece onto each of the remaining long strips. The four long binding strips should now be at least 2" (5 cm) longer than your Y measurement.

Fold the strips in half lengthwise with right sides together—this is different than a regular binding—and press.

11 Slip the petals into the fold of the binding so that the open end of each petal is flush inside the fold. Starting at the midpoint of the binding strip, work outward on either side until the section with the petals measures at least 1" (2.5 cm) less than your Y measurement. You may need to shuffle the petals around or adjust the spaces in between them. Pin the petals in place and sew down the length of the fold using a ¼" (6 mm) seam allowance, securing all of the petals as you go.

12 To attach the binding to the quilt, match one long raw edge of one binding strip with one side of the quilt, making sure the right side faces the front of the quilt. The petals must line up so that at

Silly Edges to Personalize Your Family's Happy Birthday Quilt

A petal edging isn't the only way you can bind your Happy Birthday Quilt. Switching up the edging is a great way to personalize your quilt to reflect your family's style.

You can change the shape of the petals by squaring them off or by giving them points. Make them extra skinny, extra fat, extra long, or extra short.

Check out the fussy-cut (see Tools and Techniques, page 24) tab edging in the samples—perfect for a story quilt! Fold your scraps into prairie points following the instructions in the Bright Hopes for Baby Blanket (page 152). Swap in ready-made trims such as ball fringe or rickrack or make lovely ribbon loops. If you follow the binding instructions, you can substitute whichever trims—or combination of trims—your birthday kid likes best.

When choosing your edging, keep in mind whom the quilt will be given to and how it will be used as well as the visual impact. If you choose prairie points for a bed quilt, for example, you may want to leave them off the top edge of the quilt so they won't be tickling someone in the nose while she or he sleeps. Reserve ball fringe for older children because the pom-poms could be pulled off by young children and become a choking hazard.

Edges are a great way to add whimsy and festivity to other projects also. Just insert appropriately sized petals or ribbon loops into a seam on a doll skirt or side of a pillow. Now that you've got the basics mastered, you can invent your own!

MATERIALS

* 4½ yd (4.1 m) of 45" (114.5 cm) wide white cotton or muslin for portrait blocks and handprint borders

* 2¼ yd (2 m) of mixed solid-color fabrics for portrait backgrounds

* 37' (11.3 m) of freezer paper for reinforcing fabric

* 4¼ yd (3.9 m) of backing fabric

* 80" × 80" (203 × 203 cm) square of quilt batting

* ⅞ yd (80 cm) of binding fabric for a slightly wide binding

* Coordinating thread

* Embroidery floss or yarn for tying the quilt

TOOLS

* Basic Sewing Kit

* Fabric markers in a variety of colors

* Thin-tip black fabric markers

* Painter's tape or masking tape

* Fabric paint and paintbrushes or sponges

* Palette paper or paint-mixing tray

* An assistant or two

FINISHED SIZE

This quilt is 72" (183 cm) square—perfect for a large throw, a wall quilt, or a family picnic quilt.

Community Quilt

I started making Community Quilts when my daughter was in kindergarten. I worked with her classmates to make a quilt for their teacher. It is a wonderful way to get any kind of group to work together on a special project. The children draw their own portrait blocks and print their hands on the border, and everyone can help sew.

This is also a great family project. Get the grandchildren together for a special anniversary or birthday quilt or work with all ages—aunts, uncles, and cousins—to make a wedding quilt or graduation gift.

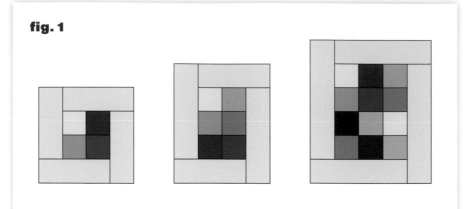

fig. 1

You may need to make adjustments to your quilt depending on how many children are participating. These instructions are for a quilt involving sixteen people, each one drawing a portrait and making handprints on the border.

Do you have more than sixteen people? Ask the older children to draw their portraits and the younger ones to make handprints. If you have fewer people and an extra square of fabric or two, use them for a message or make a square for the family pet. You can experiment with different layouts **(FIGURE 1)**, or you can change the block size to fit your project. For example, cut the sixteen blocks 10½" (26.5 cm) square to make a smaller quilt.

This project has five stages: fabric, drawing, and printing prep; drawing and printing; sewing prep; sewing; and finishing. Schedule the drawing and printing session with the entire group. If the kids want to sew with you, schedule a separate session with the group for sewing. You can also ask for help with the other stages from individual group members.

Fabric, Drawing, and Printing Prep

1 Test your fabric markers and fabric paint on your fabric. You want to be sure they look the way you want. A wash test is also a good idea. Complete these next few steps in advance, too.

2 Cut an equal number of 12 ½" (31.5 cm) squares of white cotton and 12½" (31.5 cm) squares of freezer paper.

Cut more than you will actually need. You will most certainly need extras for those who make a mistake and want to start over or who are unhappy with their first squares. For example, for a group of sixteen artists cut at least twenty squares. Most kids will be happy with their work; they are usually not nearly as nervous about drawing as adults are. Try to anticipate the needs of your particular group.

3 Place a square of freezer paper shiny side down on top of a square of fabric. Fuse the paper to the wrong side (if your fabric has a right and wrong side) by pressing with a dry iron. The paper will stabilize the fabric and make it much easier to draw on.

Using a gridded ruler and light pencil line, draw a scant ¼" (6 mm) seam allowance all the way around each square on the right side of the fabric.

Let participants know that anything they draw outside the pencil line will not show.

4 For the quilt's border, cut four strips of white cotton or muslin fabric and four strips of freezer paper. Each strip should be 12½" (31.5 cm) wide and 60½" (153.5 cm) long. Fuse the paper to the fabric as above.

Drawing and Printing

5 Inform your participants (and their parents) that the fabric markers will not wash off their clothes. You may want to provide or have them bring smocks.

Just before the drawing and printing session, tape the border strips down to a table. Arrange your paints for easy access and mix colors. Have a damp towel ready to clean hands.

6 Start the group off by having them draw their self-portraits. This project can become a wonderful lesson. For a quilt with a consistent look, ask everyone to draw a portrait of their faces from the shoulders up.

Do an Internet search of self-portrait images, check out library books, and show your group the examples. Ask them what makes a self-portrait as opposed to a regular portrait. Talk about various facial features and their placement on a person's head.

Set out the fabric markers, give each participant a square of paper-backed white fabric, and let them go to it. Try not to micromanage. It sucks the fun out and gets you nowhere.

7 As they finish their drawings, start the border printing. Print one child's hands at a time, and then have your assistant help him or her

wash up while you move on to printing with the next child. You may even want two assistants so someone can supervise the children who're still working on their portraits.

Using a brush or sponge, paint the child's palms and fingers. Position the hands and press down. Do not try to reposition the hands once they have already touched the fabric. It is better to have the handprints askew than smudged. Actually, askew prints add movement and can look very fun.

After they are all washed up, have the children write their names under their handprints with a fabric marker.

Sewing Prep

8 After the fabric markers and paints have dried, peel the freezer paper from the fabric squares, taking care not to stretch the fabric out of shape. Heat-set the markers and paint according to their instructions.

9 Cut sixteen 12½" (31.5 cm) squares of solid-color cotton fabrics in a variety of colors to suit the drawings.

Cut loosely around each portrait head, leaving about ¼" (6 mm) of space around the drawing. Machine-appliqué (see Tools and Techniques, page 21) each portrait onto the solid background.

10 Lay out the blocks of the quilt so you know where each portrait is going. You can also do this step with the kids. Talk to them about what will make a balanced quilt in terms of the color and visual weight of the various

chapter 3: celebrate

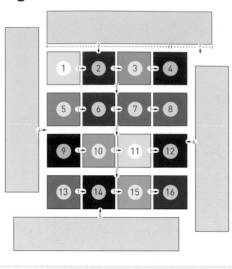

fig. 2

portraits. Or will the portraits be ordered alphabetically or by other nonvisual criteria?

Make yourself a quick sketch or take a photo of the preferred layout. Stack the squares in the order they will be sewn together with the upper left-hand square on top and the lower right-hand square on the bottom. See (**FIGURE 2**) for assembly.

Sewing the Quilt

11 If you're going to sew with kids, set up the sewing machine with two chairs. Have the iron close but in a safe area away from the activity. Ask an assistant to supervise another activity simultaneously. Only one child at a time will be able to sew with you, and you will want to have someone and something else keeping the others occupied.

12 Decide on a sewing plan based on the ages and abilities of the children in your group. While your own kids may see you sewing often and may even sew on their own, some children have never even seen a sewing machine. Letting them work the foot pedal while you steer is a good way to get them started. If they're very young, make sure they understand "start" and "stop."

13 Call the child whose block is on the top of your pile. He or she will help sew the block to the one next in the pile. Sew the first

two squares together, with the right sides of fabric together, making sure both portraits are aligned in the same direction. Be sure to open the squares up and show them how they look. Guaranteed smiles!

14 Continue stitching the blocks together with the children, adding square 3 to squares 1 and 2 and then square 4 to square 3. Repeat, making rows for squares 5-8, 9-12, and 13-16. The children whose blocks are at the end of each row will sew the rows together.

15 Finish all of the rows and press the seams to one side. Lay them out in order. The child who didn't get a chance to sew yet, whose block is at the end of row 1, will sew row 1 to row 2. The child whose block is at the end of row 2 will sew row 2 to row 3. Continue in this way until all four rows are sewn.

Now, what to do with the very last child whose block is at the end of the last row? He or she gets to help sew on the borders!

16 The borders are sewn so that each side overlaps the next. Sew the first side about three-fourths of the way to the end. Work your way counterclockwise around the center. Sew the second border piece on the full length of the quilt's center and the

Kid Work

★ Choose background fabric colors

★ Draw portraits

★ Make handprints

★ Arrange the quilt blocks

★ Sew together blocks and borders

★ Tie the quilt

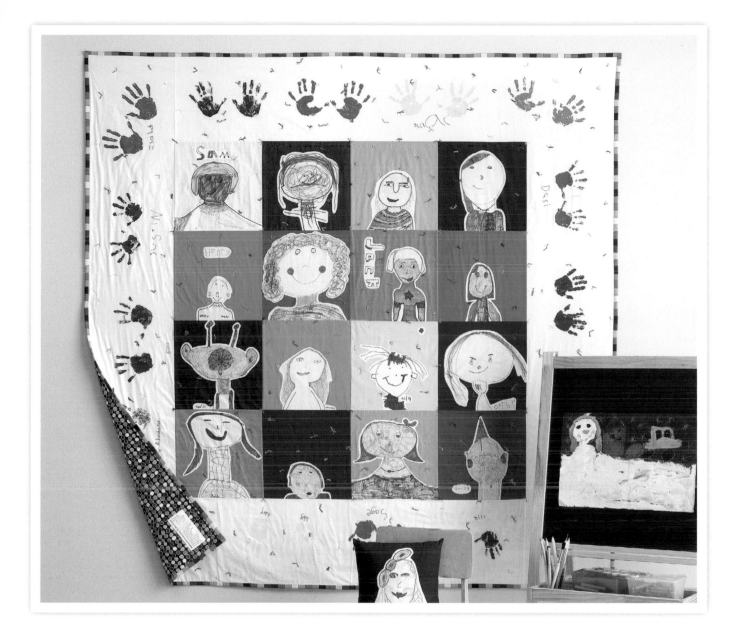

short end of the first side. Repeat this for the third and fourth sides. Finish sewing the first side.

Finishing the Quilt

17 For the Community Quilt, I am fond of tying the layers together randomly with brightly colored embroidery floss or yarn. It has a very festive confetti look! Older children have the necessary fine motor skills to help you. You can make the stitches in the quilt and the children can tie and trim the threads. Some children may be able to help with the stitching, but it can be difficult for them to push the needle and floss through so many layers. Make sure you keep this stage frustration-free—it should be exciting for them to see the quilt being finished. Keep things fun!

Alternatively, you can also machine-quilt, hand-quilt, or use a combination. For the binding, use a bright stripe and cut the strips extra wide, say, 3½" (9 cm). For this quilt I like to use a wide, brightly colored binding to create balance between the white cotton and the portraits, backgrounds, and handprints. Don't forget the label!

Variations on a Quilt

The Community Quilt has great potential for variation. I urge you to think beyond my version and create a specialized project for your family or group.

Graffiti Quilt

For older teenagers who may roll their eyes at drawing portraits and making handprints, try a graffiti quilt instead. The fabric prep will be the same. Let them doodle on the squares and border with fabric markers. You can have the fabric ready and on the tables at a sweet sixteen or graduation party or a bar or bat mitzvah. The doodling is a great party activity, and you can sew the quilt together on your own later. What a great gift for a graduate to take off to college!

If you have a more structured gathering, you may want to encourage participants to decide as a group on a theme or concept. Help them choose a topic that is appropriate to the final destination of the quilt. A gift for a friend? How about all of their favorite phrases and goofy things they say to each other. Someone moving? Try drawings of all the landmarks close by so they can take the memories with them. A grandparents' anniversary? Provide each participant with a branch of the family tree or a piece of family history to letter and illustrate.

If you have a group of teenagers who will sew the quilt, supervise the sewing but let them make the decisions and do the work themselves. With a little encouragement, teenagers are incredibly capable. As always, know your kids and prepare to be flexible. The more

they do themselves, the more invested they will be in the project.

Wheelchair or Lap Quilt

Whether you know someone in a wheelchair or are looking for a project to donate to a veterans' or nursing home, a quilt is sure to be a welcome gift. Not only will a quilt keep the recipient warm, but the cheerful drawings and handprints will make him or her smile.

Wheelchair quilts should be small enough that they don't get caught in the wheels. A 32" (81.5 cm) square or 32" × 40" (81.5 × 101.5 cm) rectangle will be safer than a larger quilt. Use an alternate layout (**FIGURE 1**, page 94), but cut the fabric for the quilt blocks 8½" (21.5 cm) square. For the layout on the left, cut four 8½" × 24½" (21.5 × 62 cm) border strips. For the middle layout, cut two short 8½" × 24½" (21.5 × 62 cm) border strips and two long 8½" × 32½" (21.5 × 82.5 cm) border strips. You can also keep the blocks at 12½" (31.5 cm), but do away with the border altogether.

Pillows from Extra Blocks

Depending on the size of your Community Quilt or the number of people you have contributing blocks, you may not be able to get all the blocks to fit right. Go ahead and curse a few times, do what you can to assemble a pleasing quilt top, and

then make simple pillows out of the rest. They will end up making the gift extra special.

A pillow is also a quick project to make with a single child as well as a wonderful introduction to a variety of techniques. Prepare two white fabric squares as above and have your child make the portrait on one and the handprints on the other. Use one square for each side of the pillow.

To make a pillow, cut out and appliqué the portrait onto a solid-color background as you would for a block for the Community Quilt. Cut another 12½" (31.5 cm) square for the back of the pillow in a contrasting color, or use a white fabric square with handprints. Pin the squares with right sides together. Sew around the outside of the pillow, leaving an opening of about 4" (10 cm) in the middle of one side. Clip the corners and turn right side out.

Press the pillow and stuff to desired fullness. Alternatively, use a purchased 12" (31.5 cm) square pillow form to stuff the pillow. Handsew the opening closed.

For a pillow with a removable cover and no handsewing to frustrate young sewers, cut two pieces for the back, 12½" × 9" (31.5 × 23 cm) each. On each piece, make a hem on one long side by folding and pressing the edge up ½" (1.3 cm) and then ½" (1.3 cm) again to enclose the raw edge. Topstitch along the inside folded edge on each piece.

With right sides together, match the raw edges of one back piece with the raw edges on one half of the front piece. Match the other back piece to the front, overlapping the two back finished edges. Pin and sew completely around the entire square. Clip corners, turn and press. Insert a 12" (30.5 cm) pillow form through the back flap.

MATERIALS

* ⅔ yd (61 cm) of quilting-weight cotton fabric for canopy top

* ⅔ yd (61 cm) of quilting-weight cotton fabric for canopy bottom

* 1¾ yd (1.6 m) of ball fringe

* ¼ yd (23 cm) of 1" (2.5 cm) wide grosgrain ribbon or a 1" × 8" (2.5 × 20.5 cm) strip of felt for spoke pockets

* ⅔ yd (61 cm) of 20" (51 cm) wide heavy interfacing for lining

* One 6" (15 cm) square felt scrap for flower detail

* Coordinating thread

* One 36" (91.5 cm) long ½" (1.3 cm) dowel for handle

* 1 round wooden or bamboo wheel joint with 8 holes from a child's construction set, like Tinker Toys

* Two 36" (91.5 cm) long ³⁄₁₆" (5 mm) dowels that fit in the wheel joint as spokes

* 1 wooden ball with ½" (1.3 cm) hole for finial

* Acrylic paint suitable for wood

* Wood glue

* 2" × 5½" × 5½" (5 × 14 × 14 cm) wooden block for stand (optional)

* Battery-operated tea lights or LED rope (optional)

continued on next page ☞

The Official Flower Dance Academy Umbrella

The Flower Umbrella Dance Academy is a wonderful place born in my daughter's imagination. Of course that big black umbrella we take to the bus stop on rainy days just wasn't cutting it. And before you ask—no, these umbrellas do not open and close. Umbrella mechanics are complicated, and we are all about sewing fun here, not frustration!

The Official Flower Dance Academy Umbrella is not only for dancing. With the simple addition of a wooden block with a hole in the middle, it becomes a whimsical centerpiece for any festive party. Drill a hole in the end of the handle and hang it upside down in a bedroom. Add a safe light to make a lantern!

TOOLS

* Basic Sewing Kit

* The Official Flower Dance Academy Umbrella patterns on side C of the insert

* Zipper foot

* Paintbrushes

* Drill or drill press with ½" (1.3 cm) drill bit

* Wood clamps

* Small handsaw or utility knife

* Fine sandpaper

FINISHED SIZE

The Official Flower Dance Academy Umbrella has an 18" (45.5 cm) canopy and a 30" (76 cm) handle.

This umbrella frame is made with minimal woodworking, but don't let that scare you away. You can do it—you are a maker! You'll cut a few dowels for the handle and the spokes, and you'll drill a single hole in the joint. If you plan to make the stand, you will need a square of wood and a hole drilled in the center. If you don't have the basic tools necessary, check with your local hardware store or lumberyard to see if they can do the cutting and drilling for you. Or hit up a handy friend or relative (thanks, Grandpa Adam!).

1 Using the pattern provided in the insert, cut one Canopy from your top fabric, one Canopy from the bottom fabric, and one Lining from the interfacing. You will have three circles with a wedge cut from each.

2 To make the lining, overlap the outer edge of the circle as indicated on the pattern, creating a wide cone. Pin the overlap and zigzag stitch down each side of the overlap, from the outer edge toward the inner point.

3 To make the pockets for the spokes of the frame, either cut eight 1" (2.5 cm) square pieces of felt or cut the 1" (2.5 cm) wide ribbon into eight 1" (2.5 cm) squares. Following the markings on the pattern, pin the eight pieces to the canopy bottom fabric. Topstitch three sides around each piece, leaving the side closest to the center point open.

4 Fold the canopy bottom in half with right sides together and match the two straight edges where the wedge was cut. Sew the two straight edges together from the outer curve to the center point, leaving the 6" (15 cm) opening as

indicated on the pattern. You will now have a floppy cone.

5 Follow the same steps for the canopy top, but do not leave the opening as you did for the canopy bottom.

6 Add some serious cuteness for your little dancer. Baste the ball fringe around the outside edge of the canopy top, keeping the pom-poms toward the center so they will hang around the outside when the umbrella is complete. Use a zipper foot to sew right next to the pom-poms.

I wanted just the pom-pom part of the ball fringe to show and not much of the woven top part, so I attached the ball fringe with the woven part over the edge of the umbrella fabric instead of sewing it flush.

7 Pin the canopy top and canopy bottom right sides together, then sew all around the outside edge. Again, a zipper foot is helpful.

Turn the umbrella canopy right side out through the hole in the canopy bottom seam. Press the canopy.

8 Roll up the canopy lining gently and insert it through the hole in the canopy bottom seam. Ease the edges out and line up the points together. You should have a very silly wide cone with ball-fringe edging and the interfacing lining as an internal structure. (You and your children may even try it on as a hat!)

To make a hole in the canopy point for the handle to go through, trim the point of the canopy top and the canopy bottom even with the hole at the point of the lining. Whipstitch the three layers together around the inner edge of the circle.

9 Using the Flower pattern, cut the flower for the finial detail from the 6" (15 cm) square scrap of felt.

Assemble the Umbrella Frame

There are four parts to the frame: the joint, the spokes, the handle, and the finial.

10 Use a Tinker Toy wheel joint that has a small hole in the center. First, enlarge this hole so the ½" (1.3 cm) dowel for the handle will slide through. Clamp the joint to a larger block of wood, a work surface, or a drill-press bed. Slowly drill a ½" (1.3 cm) hole in the center of the joint.

11 For the spokes, cut eight 7½" (19 cm) pieces of ³⁄₁₆" (5 mm) dowel with either a small handsaw or a utility knife. To use a knife, score the dowel, then snap the dowel at the score mark.

12 For the handle, cut a 36" (91.5 cm) dowel down to 30" (76 cm). I think it's a better length for kids.

Lightly sand any rough edges on all of the wooden parts.

13 Glue the spokes into the holes in the joint. Use the pattern as a guide to make sure the spokes are not crooked and are evenly spaced as they radiate out from the joint. Let the glue dry.

14 If you want to make a stand for the umbrella, use the 2" × 5½" × 5½" (5 × 14 × 14 cm) block of wood. Drill a ½" (1.3 cm) hole in the center 1½" (3.8 cm) deep.

15 Set your kids to painting the stand, the handle, the spokes, and the finial. I chose two colors for each umbrella. I used the main color for the handle, spokes, joint, and stand, and the accent color for the finial, the bottom 4" (10 cm) of the handle, and the polka dots on the base.

16 When the frame and finial are completely dry, assemble the umbrella. From underneath the canopy, ease the spokes into the pockets in the canopy. Insert the top of the handle into the joint from underneath and then up through the center hole in the canopy until it is sticking out of the hole about ½" (1.3 cm), or whatever the depth of the hole in your finial is.

17 Put the felt flower on top of the umbrella with the top of the wooden handle passing through the hole in the flower. Finish the umbrella by gluing the finial to the top of the handle and the joint to the handle. Or you can use a rubber band on the handle just underneath the joint; I used a clear elastic band.

18 To hang the umbrella like a lantern from the ceiling, drill a ⅛" (3 mm) hole through the handle ½" (1.3 cm) from its bottom. Insert a strong thread or ribbon through the hole and tie it into a loop. Hang the loop from a hook or tie it onto a ribbon garland. Set a few battery-operated tea lights inside the canopy. Read the instructions to be certain the lights are safe for your umbrella's fabric.

chapter 3: celebrate

chapter 4:
love

I know I shouldn't admit it, but this is my favorite chapter. As soon as my mother taught me to sew (thanks, Mom!), I started making dolls on her sewing machine. Dolls and animals have continued to make an appearance throughout my making life. I love that amazing moment when you have worked the twinkly eyes, the nose (if there is one!), and the sweet smile, and suddenly there is a friend. I am embarrassingly giddy making a tiny pocket or finding just the right button for a miniature coat.

When I was young, dolls and animals were my confidantes. For your children, dolls and animals will always be there, to turn to in times of joy and anger, when they are frightened and tired, never judging, always listening. There is a special responsibility in making such an important friend for a child. Take your time, and enjoy the process.

The projects in this chapter range from the simple yet sophisticated Little Smiles Bunny (page 128) to the more advanced but infinitely satisfying Hazel Doll (page 112). Alexander Lion (page 122) is a wonderfully textured gentle soul. Fun Friends from Odds and Ends (page 106) combines your precious scraps for the doll's body with your child's fanciful drawing for the face.

These are great opportunities for surprise gifts, but all of these projects have ways for kids to participate. From choosing the fabrics to helping with the stuffing, they will love seeing a new friend come to life with their help.

MATERIALS

* ¼ yd (23 cm) of fabric scraps for the body, including solid or tone-on-tone fabric for head

* 3" (7.5 cm) of rickrack or trim for pocket edge

* About forty 3–6" (7.5–15 cm) pieces of ribbon and rickrack for hair

* Cotton or polyester fill

* Coordinating thread

* Contrasting thread or embroidery floss for face

* Scrap of cotton batting (optional)

* Several small buttons for dress details (optional)

TOOLS

* Basic Sewing Kit

* Fun Friends from Odds and Ends patterns on side A of insert

* Child's drawing of a face

* Darning or free-motion foot

FINISHED SIZE

Fun Friends are 15" (38 cm) from head to toe, not including their hair.

Fun Friends from Odds and Ends

Since I started designing quilts, I have accumulated huge bags of scraps. I can't seem to throw out any of them, even the smallest crumbs. In addition to not being wasteful, I think so many of the colors and patterns are just wonderful and remind me of the original quilt they were used for. These Fun Friends are perfect for using up those fabulous scraps. You can even make a doll to match the quilt the scraps came from.

Using a child's drawing of a face makes each doll even more unique. The scrappy piecing and whimsical features are made for each other. The integrated pocket is an added bonus and just right for special surprises, love notes, or a gift from the tooth fairy!

For these dolls I like to use free-motion machine embroidery for the faces. The lines are more expressive than controlled hand embroidery, just like your child's original drawings. You can, of course, hand-embroider the faces if you prefer. Whichever technique you use, peruse your child's drawings to find a simple yet playful face that fits the style of these dolls.

I like to use one color thread for all of the features when making Fun Friends to highlight the expressiveness of the face. It's also quicker and fits with the "quick, let's whip up a doll" nature of this project. Choose a thread or embroidery-floss color that will contrast with the head fabric but that will coordinate with the scraps you use for the dress. So, for light fabrics try dark brown, dark gray, or dark blue thread. For dark fabrics try pale yellow or off-white thread. You can, of course, change colors for various features if you wish. If you are hand-embroidering, use a simple backstitch (see Tools and Techniques, page 20).

The pocket on these Fun Friends is sewn right into the scrappy piecing for the dress. You make the pocket first so you can place it where you want within the piecing.

1 Make the pocket front by cutting two Pocket pieces (see pattern insert) from scraps. On the long side of one piece, baste a scrap of rickrack to the right side so the center length of the rickrack is ¼" (6 mm) from the raw edge. Pin the pocket pieces together with right sides facing. Sew along the edge with the rickrack, stitching down the center length of the rickrack, then turn the pocket wrong sides together so the rickrack creates a decorative edge. This becomes the top of the pocket.

2 For the back of the pocket, cut a scrap of fabric as wide as the pocket and at least 2¾" (7 cm) tall. Lay the pocket on the right side of this backing piece so the bottom edge of the pocket matches a 2¾" (7 cm) side of the backing. Stitch the pocket to the backing ⅛" (3 mm) from the raw edge. Treat the pocket as one scrap when you are piecing the front of the dress **(FIGURE 1)**.

3 Make the Fun Friend's dress next. Randomly piece together the pocket and other scraps to create a single piece that is slightly larger than the Dress pattern. Be sure to position the pocket near the center with the opening facing up.

Make another patched piece for the back of the dress. Cut out the Dress pieces using the pattern.

4 Choose narrow scraps for piecing the Fun Friend's arms and legs and cut them into lengths of about 4" (10 cm). Sew together the long edges to make two pieces about 4" × 6" (10 × 15 cm) for the

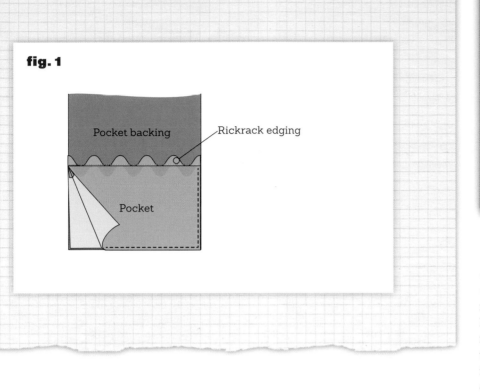

fig. 1

Pocket backing

Rickrack edging

Pocket

arms and two pieces about 4" × 9" (10 × 23 cm) for the legs. Fold each of the four pieces in half lengthwise and, using the patterns, cut two Arms and two Legs. You can also make the arms and legs out of single large scraps.

5 With right sides together, sew the arms and legs down the long side, around the curve, and up the other side, leaving the short straight edge open. Clip the curves and turn right side out, smoothing the seams from the inside. Press the arms and legs.

6 Stuff the arms and legs, but leave the top ½" (1.3 cm) unstuffed so that they can be attached to the body.

Make the Doll's Head

7 Start with the face by cutting one piece of the fabric you're using for the head and one piece of batting 5" × 5" (12.5 × 12.5 cm).

Place the fabric on top of the batting and press to have them stick lightly together. The batting gives the face a slightly quilted look, but it's optional.

8 Trace the outline of the Head pattern on the fabric. Enlarge or shrink your child's drawing to fit on the front of the head, then transfer the face onto the fabric. Machine- or hand-embroider the eyes, nose, and mouth, or whatever fun features your child has come up with.

9 Cut out the Front Head along the line, then trim the batting away from the seam allowance. Using the pattern, cut another Head piece for the back of the head.

10 Create the doll's body by sewing the head pieces to the dress pieces. Sew the front head piece to the front dress along the straight side of the head and short side of the dress, right sides together. Do the same with the backs of the head and dress.

11 Make the Fun Friend's hair. Cut the hair ribbon and rick-rack into 3–6" (7.5–15 cm) lengths. Fold the pieces in half, matching raw ends. Group two or three pieces together and baste them to the front of the head, matching ribbon or rickrack ends to the raw edge of the fabric. Make sure the loops are turned toward the inside of the head (**FIGURE 2**, page 110).

Assemble the Doll

12 Pin the arms and legs to the dress front where indicated on the pattern, matching the raw edges. Starting where the head and dress meet, sew the doll's left arm to the dress front, stitching ⅛" (3mm) from the edge. Continue stitching down the side of the dress. Turn the corner at the bottom and sew on the legs. Continue up the other side of the dress and attach the doll's right arm.

13 With right sides together, pin the front and back together. Check that the arms, legs, and hair are inside the doll. Sew around the entire doll, leaving the opening for turning and stuffing as indicated on the pattern.

14 Clip the head curves and the bottom dress corners. Turn

fig. 2

Pocket

the doll right side out, smoothing the seams from the inside. Press, being careful to keep the iron away from the ribbon or rickrack.

15 Stuff the head and body to the desired firmness. Sew the opening closed by hand.

16 If your Fun Friend is for a child more than three years old, you can add some extra fun with a few small buttons. Choose a variety of sizes and colors to coordinate with your doll and sew them firmly onto the dress or in the hair.

MATERIALS

* ¾ yd (68.5 cm) of cotton, cotton/linen, or linen fabric for body
* Cotton fabric scraps for underwear
* Cotton fabric scraps for hair
* 4" × 5" (10 × 12.5 cm) piece of muslin for nose facing
* Coordinating thread
* Embroidery floss for face
* Cotton or polyester fill
* A handful of gravel and a 4" × 6" (10 × 15 cm) scrap each of muslin and batting for weighting (optional)
* Green felt scraps for hair decoration (optional)
* Buttons, sequins, and beads for hair decoration (optional)

TOOLS

* Basic Sewing Kit
* Hazel Doll patterns on sides A, B, C, and D of the insert

FINISHED SIZE

Hazel Doll is 28" (71 cm) tall.

Hazel Doll

I got my start as a maker by sewing dolls, and they are still a favorite of mine to make. Draw a face on even the simplest of stuffed forms, and magic happens. I have adapted the nose for this doll from a technique I learned from soft sculptor Dorothy Lazara while I was her apprentice many years ago.

This doll is just right for hugging, sits nicely at tea parties, and plays well with other dolls. And Hazel's wardrobe is easier to sew than it looks! The skirt and shirt are reversible so you only have to make one of each to have dressing options. The coat is one-piece easy, and the shoes are two simple shapes. Customize them all with trims, buttons, and embroidery for endless possibilities. I have named her Hazel after my older daughter, but you—and your child—must, of course, give your doll her own name.

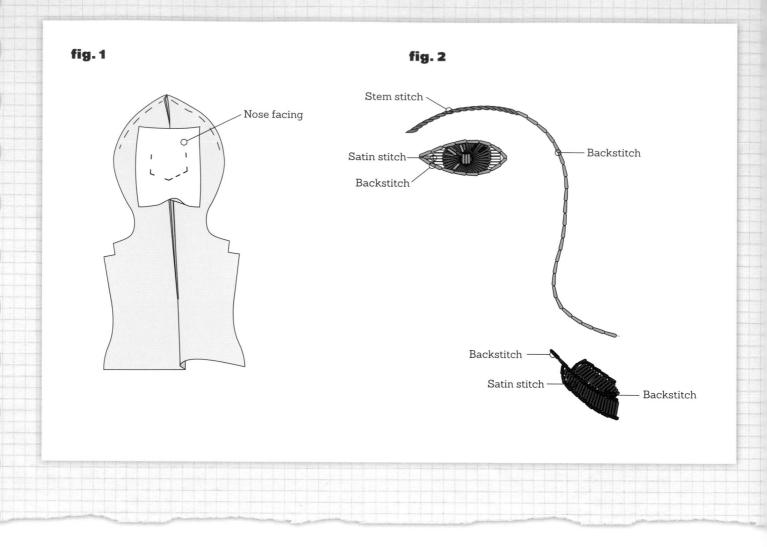

fig. 1

Nose facing

fig. 2

Stem stitch

Satin stitch

Backstitch

Backstitch

Backstitch

Satin stitch

Backstitch

Take your time sewing Hazel, especially on the tight curves like the thumb and the important curves like the nose. Unless you are planning to turn her into a warty witch, you will want to make the nose seam and rest of the face as smooth as possible; handsew using a backstitch to give you more control if you prefer.

1 Fold skin fabric in half, matching the selvedges, and cut body pieces according to the Body Front, Body Back, Leg, Arm, and Ear patterns (see insert). Transfer all markings to the body pieces, noting where to leave openings and how to

embroider her facial features. Cut two Front Underwear pieces and two Back Underwear pieces from the underwear fabric. Cut two Front Hair pieces and two Back Hair pieces from the hair fabric.

2 Position the hair pieces on the head pieces right sides up. Baste them in place where the raw edges of the hair meet the raw edges of the head. Turn under the remaining edges of the hair ⅛" (3 mm) and appliqué the hair to the head.

Sew the Body

Hazel Doll's underwear is an integral part of her body. The instructions to make the rest of her wardrobe are in the sidebar on page 118.

3 With right sides together, sew the arms and the legs. Leave the openings on the side seams for stuffing and on the tops where they will be sewn to the body.

4 Sew darts on the back Underwear, following the pattern.

the nose facing to the inside of the face (**FIGURE 1**). Remove pins.

Using three strands of embroidery floss that match your skin fabric, backstitch by hand along the line that defines the nose.

Remove the basting stitches and stuff the nose.

9 Embroider the rest of the face as you like, following the markings transferred from the pattern or creating your own features (**FIGURE 2**). For the eyes, I used embroidery floss in white, black for the pupil, and several coordinating colors plus a highlight and a shadow color for the irises. For the eyebrows, I chose floss that matches the hair. The stem stitch I used for the eyebrows is similar to a backstitch, but the stitches are angled and overlap each other to create a thicker line. For the lips, I used several coordinating colors plus a highlight and a shadow color.

Finish the Body

10 Baste the ears to the front of the head as indicated on the pattern, matching raw edges.

11 Open the top openings of the legs and match the front and back seams together. This flattens the top of the legs and forces the feet to face forward. Baste the legs to the front of the body as indicated on the pattern, matching raw edges. Make sure the feet will face forward!

12 Pin or baste the front and back body pieces together, carefully matching raw edges and keeping the ears and legs tucked inside. Sew around the entire body, except for the notches cut out for the arms.

Lay out the front and back body parts and underwear parts. With right sides together, sew underwear sections to body sections.

5 With right sides together, match the center back seams of the body and sew, leaving an opening for turning and stuffing.

6 With right sides together, match the center front seams of the doll and sew.

Clip the curved seams. Turn the arms and legs right side out and press. For the front and back of the doll, smooth the seams and press using the tip of your iron to get inside the nose and other curves.

7 Now make the ears. Sew the ears around the curved side, leaving the flat side open. Trim the seam allowance to ⅛" (3 mm) to reduce bulk. Clip and turn the ears. Finally, smooth the seams from the inside and press the ears flat.

Make the Face

8 Lay the nose facing on the inside of the face, keeping the nose sticking out (do not flatten the face into the nose facing). Pin the doll's face to the facing just below the nose and in the middle of the forehead. You are creating a pocket for the nose so it can be stuffed from the inside between the eyebrows. Baste

fig. 3   **fig. 4**

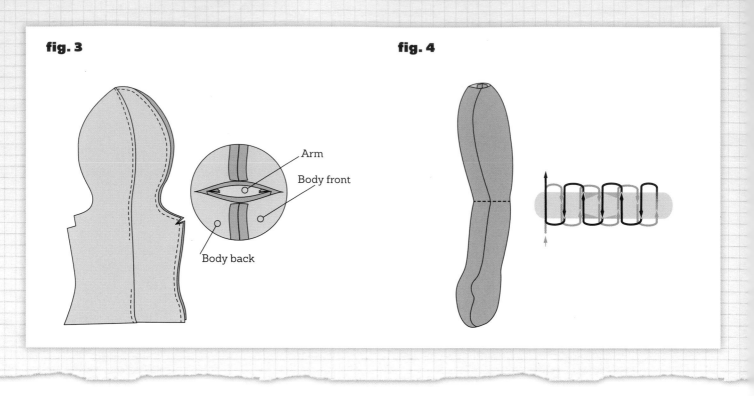

Arm

Body front

Body back

13 Insert the arms through the opening in the back. Flatten the shoulder notches so the sewn seams are together. Match the raw edges of the arms with the edges of the notches, making sure that the thumbs are facing forward **(FIGURE 3)**.

14 Sew the shoulder seam. Sew again ⅛" (3 mm) from the first seam toward the outside to reinforce the arms.

15 Clip around the entire body and turn. Smooth seams from the inside and press.

16 Stuff the doll starting with the head.

To make your doll sit nicely on her own, you can add a bit of weight to the front of the torso. Cut a scrap of muslin 4" × 6" (10 × 15 cm) and fold it in half widthwise. Sew two of the sides closed and fill the pocket with gravel. Sew the remaining side closed.

Wrap the pillow in a scrap of batting and secure it with a few stitches. Insert the pillow into the lower front torso of the doll.

Stuff the rest of the body. Sew the back opening closed by hand.

17 Stuff the arms and legs from the hands to the elbow joint and the feet to the knee joint. Match sewn seams on the front and back of each leg at the knees and front and back of each arm at the elbows. Hand- or machine sew across the joints so they will be able to bend. If you handsew, make a running stitch with floss across the joint and then back again, sewing through the same holes but in reverse; this fills in the blanks made from the first running stitch **(FIGURE 4)**.

Stuff the rest of each arm and leg and handsew the openings closed.

Now, sit her next to you on the edge of the table and have a little chat.

Ask her what she would like you to do with her hair.

Finish the Hair

18 Follow one of the project photographs for sewing the hair or design your own.

Consider the center head seam as the hair part and decide where the hair is going to flow off the head. For example, if your doll will have two braids, decide if the braids will start high on her head, above her ears, or lower down. This spot on the head will be called the base.

19 Choose several skeins of embroidery floss in colors lighter and darker than the hair fabric. Using three strands of embroidery floss, start a running stitch at the base. Leave a tail as long as you would like the braid to be, plus a few inches for take-up within the braid and trimming at the bottom.

Make a running stitch up to a point in the part. Stitch back down about ⅛–¼" (3–6 mm) next to the first row and come back out at the base near where you went in. Leave another tail and cut the floss.

20 With new pieces of floss, continue to sew the hair, radiating out from the base and toward the center part or edges of fabric hair.

There will be empty triangular areas between the pieces of floss. For these areas, fill in with M-shaped stitches. Start at the base, sew to the outer edge, and then sew part of the way back to the base and then back again to the edge. You may need to do this a few times depending on the size of the triangular area. Sew back to the base and leave a tail.

21 After you have finished covering the hair fabric with stitches, check out the tail of floss coming off the head. This will become one of the braids (or a bun or ponytail if you prefer). If you would like to make it a bit thicker, you can add threads by taking a single stitch at the base and leaving a tail on both sides.

22 To make plaits, divide the tail into three sections and braid. Tie the ends with floss.

Alternatively, twist the tail and then coil it around into a bun. Tuck in the ends and pin in place. With matching floss, start at the outside where you have tucked in the ends and make whipstitches over the coil about every ¼–½" (6 mm–1.3 cm). Work your way around the bun toward the center.

23 You can make a flower for the doll's hair with sequins, if you like. Cut two small leaf shapes from felt. Sew a backstitch down the center of each leaf with contrasting thread. Layer three or four sequins, smallest on top. Sew through the sequins largest to smallest and through a bead. Go back down through the sequins. Sew the leaves onto the hair and sew the flower on top of the leaves. (Or, use the Flower pattern provided for the Sew Sweet Strawberry Bag, side B on the insert.) Sew a button or sequins and a bead in the center, then sew the flower to the doll's hair.

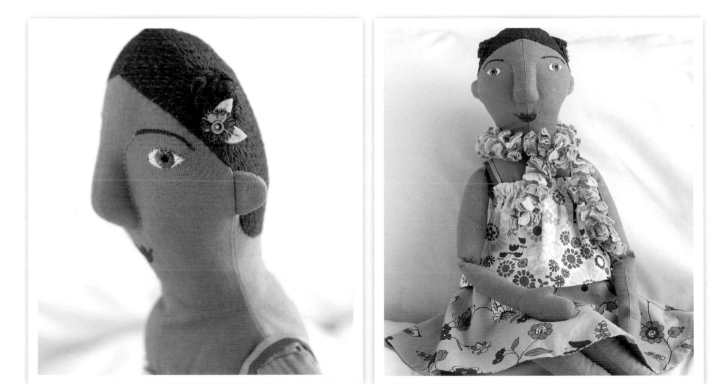

Stitching Hazel Doll's Wardrobe

Now for the really fun part: a reversible shirt and skirt and a coordinated coat! I cannot pass up any opportunity for shoes with flowers on them. Feel free to make these shoes without them for speed and simplicity, but I dare you to resist this lovely touch. And—get ready for this—miniature Laugh at Yourself Slippers, Instant Drama Chenille Boa, and Ladybug Cape all for your doll to coordinate with the full-size versions you make for your child!

MATERIALS

For the skirt:
* ⅓ yd (30.5 cm) each of two different quilting cottons (⅔ yd [61 cm] total)

* 17½" (44.5 cm) of extra-wide double-fold bias tape

* 13" (33 cm) of ¼" (6 mm) or ⅜" (1 cm) wide elastic

* Coordinating thread

* Trim (optional)

For the shirt:
* ¼ yd (23 cm) each of two different quilting cottons (½ yd [45.5 cm] total)

* Two pieces of reversible ribbon, each 4½" (11.5 cm) long

* 12" (30.5 cm) of ¼" (6 mm) or ⅜" (1 cm) elastic

* Coordinating thread

For the coat:
* 20" × 22" (51 × 56 cm) piece of loosely woven wool, wool bouclé, or other midweight coating fabric or felt

* Trim and embroidery floss

* One ½–⅝" (1.3–1.5 cm) button with shank

* 2½" (6.5 cm) piece of round elastic or hair band

* Coordinating thread

* A child's drawing to embroider on the coat (optional)

* Trim (optional)

For the shoes:
* Felt scraps, one color for uppers and one color for soles

* Coordinating thread

* Embroidery floss (optional)

* A pinch of flower and circle sequins (optional)

* A pinch of beads (optional)

* Green felt scrap for leaves (optional)

For mini Laugh at Yourself Slippers:
* Felt scraps, one color for uppers and one color for soles

* Coordinating thread

* Buttons, bells, or other trims (optional)

For a mini Instant Drama Chenille Boa:
* 24" (61 cm) of ¼" (6 mm) or ⅜" (1 cm) ribbon

* ⅛ yd (11.5 cm) each of four colors of flannel (½ yd [45.5 cm] of flannel total)

* Coordinating thread

For a mini Ladybug Cape:
* 12" (30.5 cm) square of red felt

* Scrap of black felt

* 11½" (29 cm) of ⅜" (1 cm) double-fold bias tape

* Scrap of Velcro

* Coordinating thread

fig. 1

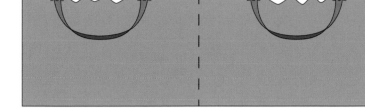

fig. 2

Cut.

TOOLS

∗ Basic Sewing Kit

∗ Hazel Doll wardrobe patterns on sides A, B, and D of the insert

Make the Skirt

① Using the pattern, cut four Skirt pieces, two each from two different fabrics. This will make the skirt reversible. With one matching set (A), place right sides together and sew the two straight side seams. Repeat with the other matching set (B). Turn A right sides out.

② If you would like to add rickrack (or other trim) to the bottom of the skirt, baste it to the front bottom edge of A so that the center line of the rickrack is ¼" (6 mm) away from the raw edge of the skirt.

③ Place A inside B with right sides together and match side seams and raw edges. Stitch together around the hem. Turn right sides out. Press the skirt.

④ Open the two ends of the bias tape. With right sides together, match the ends and sew halfway across the width. This will create an opening for threading the elastic through the waistband. Open the narrow side

of the bias tape and, matching raw edges, pin to the waist of the skirt. Sew the bias tape along the fold closest to the raw edge all around the waist.

⑤ Fold the bias tape over the waist, enclosing the raw edge. Topstitch along the narrow side of the bias tape, catching the wide edge in on the back as you sew. Then, thread the elastic through the opening in the bias tape, around the waist, and back out the opening. Overlap the elastic ends and sew them together. Tuck the elastic into the opening and sew the opening closed.

Make the Shirt

① Using the pattern, cut two Shirt pieces, one each from two different fabrics. This makes it reversible for multiple wardrobe possibilities! Pin the ribbon straps to the right side of one piece (A), where indicated on the pattern, matching one end of the ribbon to the raw edge of the fabric and looping the ribbon so the other end matches the raw edge of the fabric. The ribbon is shorter than the fabric between the two ends, so the fabric will hang loose. Baste the ribbon ends **(FIGURE 1)**.

② With right sides together, match the two short ends of A and sew. Next, with right sides together, match the two short ends of B and sew, leaving the section open as indicated to thread the elastic through.

③ On both A and B, fold up the bottom ½" (1.3 cm) and press. Fold up another ½" (1.3 cm) to make a finished hem. Topstitch the hems on A and B.

④ Turn B right side out. Insert B into A with right sides together and matching the back seams. Sew around the top edge. Because of the short length of the ribbon, you will have to shift the fabric as you go to keep both sides matched.

⑤ Turn the shirt right sides out and wrong sides together. Press.

⑥ To make the casing for the elastic, stitch ⅝" (1.5 cm) from the top edge of the shirt. Thread the elastic through the hole made in the back seam of B, through the casing, and out the hole. Overlap the elastic ends and sew them together. Tuck the elastic into the opening and handsew the opening closed.

chapter 4: love ♥

stitch. Sew each shoe upper onto the sole with a whipstitch.

② To make fancy sequin flowers, cut two small leaves from green felt. Using a double strand of sewing thread or floss, backstitch a stem onto the shoe starting from the bottom of the stem. At the top of the stem, thread a stack of three or four sequins, largest to smallest. Add a bead and go back down through the stack of sequins. Come back up part way down the stem and sew on a second stack of sequins and a bead. Come up again near the bottom of the stem and sew on the leaf by backstitching about three-fourths of the way up the center of the leaf. Secure the thread on the inside of the shoe. Repeat as a mirror image on the other shoe. Or instead, you could add tiny buttons.

Make the Coat

① Fold the fabric in half and place the pattern on the fold where indicated. Cut Coat on fold of fabric. Following the pattern, cut through the fold on the front of the coat.

② Topstitch along the sleeve cuffs ¼" (6 mm) from the edge. Refold the coat so that the open front edges butt together and the right sides of the fabric are inside. Then, sew the underarm seams.

③ Turn coat right side out and press.

④ Topstitch ¼" (6 mm) from the edge along the raw edges on the bottom, front opening, and neck. If you are using a loosely woven fabric, you can pull out the threads along the edges to create a fringe, if desired.

⑤ If desired, make lapels by folding the coat front as indicated on the pattern and pressing.

⑥ To add a closure, fold elastic in half and sew the ends securely to the front of the coat as marked on the pattern. Cut a ½" (1.3 cm) square of matching felt or cut from the same fabric and sew it over the elastic ends. Sew a button on the opposite side of the coat front.

⑦ Add trim along the bottom of the coat if desired or an embroidered design based on your child's drawing. Extra-special embroidery makes this simple coat unique. Copy your child's drawing to the appropriate size and transfer it onto the coat. (See Tools and Techniques, page 16.) Embroider the design as desired.

Make the Shoes

① Following the pattern, cut two Shoe Soles and two Shoe Uppers. Match the two straight seams on each shoe upper to form the heel and

Make Mini Laugh at Yourself Slippers

① Using the patterns from the insert, cut two Shoe Soles and four Shoe Uppers from felt.

② Match two shoe uppers and sew them together along the top front curve. Match the remaining two uppers and sew the top front curve. Then, match the two straight seams on each shoe to form the heel and sew.

③ Sew each shoe upper onto the sole with a whipstitch. Add buttons, flowers, or bells if desired.

Make a Mini Instant Drama Chenille Boa

① Seal the two ribbon ends. (See "Working with Ribbon" in Tools and Techniques, page 19).

② From each color of flannel, cut two strips from selvedge to selvedge that are 1½" (3.8 cm) wide. Layer the flannels into two stacks with four lengths each. Cut the strips at a 45-degree angle and ½" (1.3 cm) apart along the entire length of each stack. Snip off the points on either end of the stacks to square them off (**FIGURE 2**, page 119).

③ Starting 1" (2.5 cm) in from one end of the ribbon, place one strip stack perpendicular and under the ribbon and one strip stack perpendicular and on top of the ribbon. The center of the strip should match the center of the ribbon. Start sewing straight down the middle of the ribbon, adding adjacent strips under and on top of the ribbon as you go. Continue sewing strip stacks onto the ribbon until you are 1" (2.5 cm) from the other end of the ribbon.

④ Put the boa in a mesh lingerie bag or pillowcase so it doesn't get lost in the washer. Machine-wash and dry. Repeat if the boa's not fluffy enough.

Make a Mini Ladybug Cape

① Using the patterns, cut two Ladybug Cape pieces from red felt. Cut four Ladybug Spots from black felt. Hand- or machine-appliqué the black spots onto the wings. Place the wings right side up and next to each other.

② Open the bias tape and fold in half widthwise to find the center. Pin the bias tape to the front of the wings with one wing on either side of the center, matching the raw edge of the narrow side of the bias tape with the neck edge of the wings. Stitch along the bias tape in the fold closest to the raw edge of the narrow side of the tape, attaching it to the wings.

③ Fold the bias tape over the neck edge and tuck in the two short ends. If machine sewing, topstitch the tape, starting with one short end. Continue along the entire length of the bias tape and turn to finish the other short end. Make sure you catch in the back side of the tape. You can also handsew the bias tape.

④ Cut a small square of Velcro and sew one square to each end of the bias tape so they will stick when overlapped.

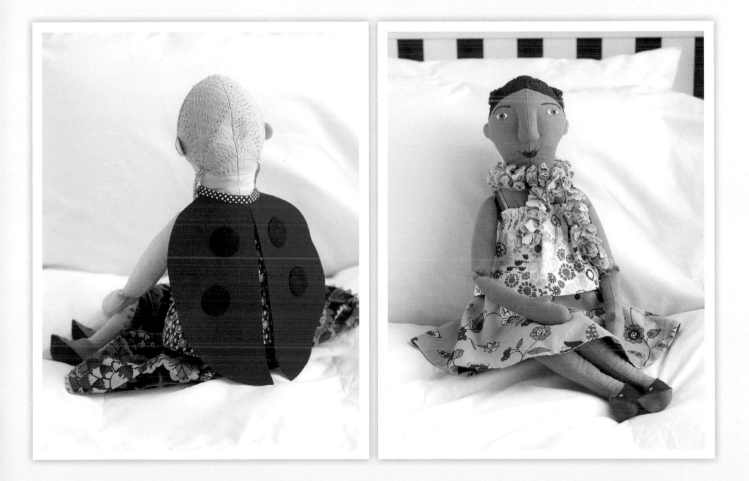

Alexander Lion

When I was little, my stuffed animals were some of my best friends. Among many others, I had a lion named Sunshine who was a wise and gentle listener. Lions in particular seem to be that way, making them a special friend to make for any child. A lion is also a great opportunity to have fun with a variety of textures: one for the body, one for the mane, and another for the ears and nose. The first lion I actually made was for my cousin's son, Alexander, so this lion is named for him.

MATERIALS

* ½ yd (45.5 cm) of textured fabric such as velveteen, wool, low pile fur, or tweed for body
* Scraps of contrasting fabric for ear interiors and nose
* 7" (18 cm) of ⅜"–½" (1–1.3 cm) wide ribbon for tail
* ¼ yd (23 cm) each of four different flannels for tail and mane (1 yd [91.5 cm] total)
* Embroidery floss for mouth
* Two ½" (1.3 cm) buttons for eyes
* Cotton or polyester fill
* Coordinating thread

TOOLS

* Basic Sewing Kit
* Alexander Lion patterns on side A of the insert
* Walking foot

FINISHED SIZE

Alexander Lion is 7" × 14" × 15" (18 × 35.5 × 38 cm).

Alexander Lion is another great project for hunting through thrift stores (or your stash) for cool fabrics. You could repurpose a thrifted tweed blazer for his body and incorporate interesting lightweight fabrics, such as linen, in his ears. Chenille is perfect for Alexander's mane and tail. If you have already tried the Instant Drama Chenille Boa (page 40), making the mane and tail will be a snap. If not, now is the time to find out how easy and fun making chenille is. Also, you can embroider his eyes if you don't want to use buttons.

1 Using the pattern from the insert, cut two Body pieces, one Underbody piece, two Ears, and eight Legs from body fabric. Also cut two Ears and one Nose piece from contrasting scraps.

2 With right sides together, match legs to create four sets. Stitch around the outside of each leg, leaving the top of each leg open for turning and stuffing. Next, clip the curved edges of the legs, turn right side out, and stuff. Leave the part of the leg near the opening unstuffed.

3 To make the nose, fold the nose in half into a rectangle. Fold down the two corners on the folded side to meet in the center of the open side. You will now have a triangle. Press the nose. Baste along the long open side of the triangle **(FIGURE 1a)**.

4 Baste the legs to the body pieces (two legs on each piece, of course) where indicated on the pattern, matching the raw edges so the legs will be inside when you sew the body together.

5 Match one long side of the underbody piece to one body piece at points A and B, then sew from A to B. Then match the other long side of the underbody to the remaining body piece and sew from A to B, leaving the opening for turning as indicated.

6 Match the remaining long edges of the body pieces along Alexander's back and under his chin. This gets a little tricky with the stuffed legs inside, so shift them around and have one or two poke out the turning opening. Stitch the seam, leaving open the notch for the tail and the notch for the nose.

7 Insert the ribbon for the tail into the tail notch so that about 1" (2.5 cm) of the tail is sticking out and the rest of the ribbon is inside the body. Flatten the opening so that the back body seam is centered in between the two underbody seams. Stitch across the tail notch.

8 For the nose, flatten the nose notch so the back body seam and chin seam are matching. Make a ⅛" (3 mm) clip on each folded side, allowing the triangle nose to fit in the notch. Insert the nose so that the open folds are facing the chin seam and the raw edges are matching. Stitch across the nose notch **(FIGURE 1b)**.

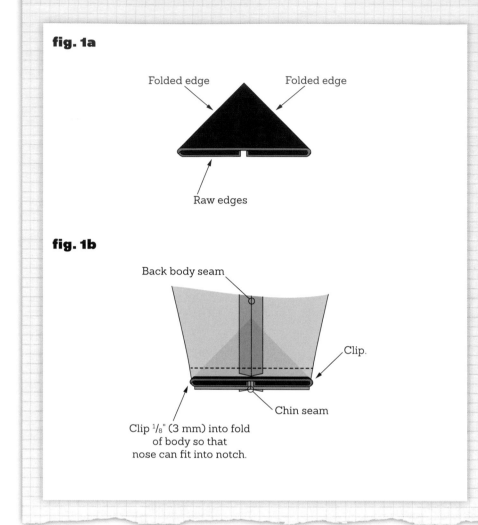

fig. 1a

Folded edge   Folded edge

Raw edges

fig. 1b

Back body seam

Clip.

Chin seam

Clip ⅛" (3 mm) into fold of body so that nose can fit into notch.

9 Clip the curved body seams and turn the body right side out. Then stuff the body and sew the opening closed by hand.

Construct the Mane and Tail

10 Cut the four colors of flannel into bias strips 8" (20.5 cm) wide. Make a continuous strip of each color by overlapping the ends of each bias strip on the diagonal about ½" (1.3 cm) with right sides up. Sew with a wide zigzag stitch.

You also need one piece of one color cut 1½" × 1¾" (3.8 × 4.5 cm) for the base of the tail and one strip of another color cut 1 ½" × 15" (3.8 × 38 cm) for the base of the mane. This can also be pieced to make a continuous strip.

11 Stack the four 8" (20.5 cm) wide strips on top of each other, aligning the edges. Pin.

Starting on one long edge, sew the entire length of the stack of flannel ⅜" (1 cm) from the edge. Then sew subsequent rows ⅝" (1.5 cm) from the previous one. Continue until the entire stack of flannels is sewn. If your walking foot does not have a stitch guide to help sew the ⅝" (1.5 cm) rows, mark the rows before you sew. You can also eyeball the rows; chenille is very forgiving!

Kid Work

★ Choose colors and fabrics
★ Wash and dry the chenille mane and tail
★ Stuff Alexander Lion

12 Cut the long stitched stack widthwise into four 8" (20.5 cm) sections. Cut between the stitched rows, making forty-two ⅝"× 8" (1.5 × 20.5 cm) strips. You will need forty strips for the mane and two for the tail.

13 Then, construct the mane, using the 1½" × 15" (3.8 × 38 cm) strip as the base. With the right side of the flannel facing up and starting 1" (2.5 cm) from the end and ¼" (6 mm) from the edge, sew twenty strips down along the side until you are 1" (2.5 cm) from the other end. Shift the strips to the right so that about 5" (12.5 cm) are to the right of the stitching and about 3" (7.5 cm) are to the left. Stagger the strips by varying the measurement on each side by about ½–¾" (1.3–2 cm) **(FIGURE 2)**.

14 Turn the mane over so the wrong side of the flannel is up and the first row of strips is flipped out of the way to the left. Starting 1" (2.5 cm) in from the end

and ¼" (6 mm) from the edge, sew another twenty strips down along the side until you are 1" (2.5 cm) from the other end. Shift the strips to the right as with the first row, again staggering the strips.

15 For the end of the tail, sew the remaining two strips to the 1 ½" × 1¾" (3.8 × 4.5 cm) piece of flannel **(FIGURE 3)**. Stitch them down near the center of each strip, making four pieces for the tail. Shift the strips slightly so that the four ends are not all the same length.

16 Wash the mane and tail end in the washer and dryer to make them fluffy. Put the tail end in a mesh lingerie bag or a pillowcase so it doesn't disappear in the wash.

17 Pinch the right-hand side of the mane base flannel down the length about ½" (1.3 cm) from the raw edge and ¼" (6 mm) from the first row of strips you sewed **(FIGURE 4)**.

Finish Alexander Lion

18 Match the pinched fold with the mane line as noted on the pattern. The 1" (2.5 cm) on each end without strips will hang free under Alexander's chin. Sew the mane onto the head at the fold.

19 Fold in the two long edges of the tail base and then fold the tail base in half widthwise. Tuck the end of the ribbon tail into

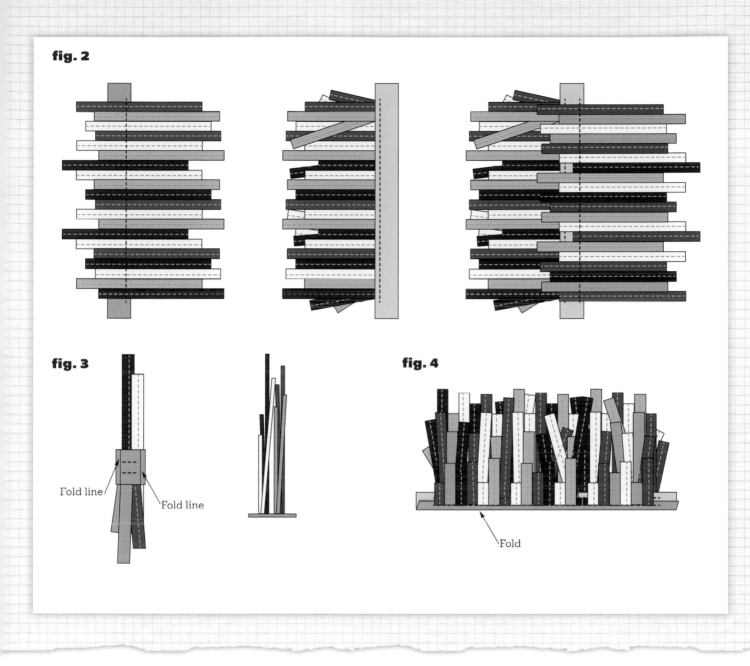

fig. 2

fig. 3

Fold line

Fold line

fig. 4

Fold

the pocket that you just created and sew securely.

20 For the ears, match one ear cut from body fabric and one ear cut from contrasting fabric with right sides together. Sew the long curved edge of each ear, leaving the straight side open for turning. Clip the curves, turn, and press. Then turn under the raw edges of the ears

and handsew them to the head as indicated on the pattern.

21 Flip the nose up and stuff it with a bit of polyester stuffing through the slit you made when you folded the triangle. Sew the slit closed, then flip the nose back down and tack the point of the nose in place with a few stitches.

22 Embroider the mouth as indicated on the pattern. Start on one side at the corner of the mouth. Follow the line up to the point of the nose and then back down to the corner of the mouth on the other side to form the W shape.

23 For the eyes, sew on brown or black buttons. Or, you can embroider them if Alexander Lion will be given to a young child.

Little Smiles Bunny

Sew cute! Sew quick! This is a great little present for a newborn, and it's fun to bundle with the Bright Hopes for Baby Blanket (page 152). The arms and legs are just the right size for little hands to grab. You can make this bunny from quilting-weight cotton, but also try soft cotton twill, wool, or linen. Just make sure your fabric is woven densely enough to withstand tightly sewn curves and lots of baby love.

Make sure all of the seams and the bunny's features are securely sewn for safety. You can strengthen your stitches by using a shorter stitch length and double-stitching the seams.

1 Cut one Front Body piece and two Back Body pieces using the pattern. Also cut two Ears from the body fabric and two from the inner ear fabric.

2 Embroider the face as shown on the pattern or experiment with your own design. Use a satin stitch (see Tools and Techniques, page 20) for the nose and a few quick stitches for the eyes.

3 Match one outer ear piece with one inner ear piece, right sides together. Sew around the curve of the ear, leaving the straight end open. Repeat with the other ear. Clip the curves, turn the ears right side out, and press the seams.

Fold the bottom of the ear over with the inner ear inside. Pin the ears to the front body piece where indicated, raw edges together and ears facing inward, and baste them to the head.

4 Make the bunny tail. Cut the ribbon into three pieces about 2½" (6.5 cm) long each or use one piece of wider ribbon. Fold each piece so the raw ends are matching. Baste the ribbons to the back body piece where indicated, matching the raw edges of the ribbon to the raw edges of the fabric.

5 Match the two back body pieces with right sides together. Sew the center back seam, leaving the opening for turning as indicated. Pin the front and back body pieces right sides together, keeping the tail and ears inside. Sew around the entire outside of the bunny.

6 Clip the seam allowances carefully all the way around. Turn the bunny right sides out, smoothing the seams from the inside, and press. Stuff the bunny and sew the opening closed.

Kid Work

★ Choose the fabrics
★ Stuff the Little Smiles Bunny

chapter 4: love ♥

chapter 5:
rest

In 2003, my mother and I started the Bright Hopes Collaborative Quilt Project to give children without a permanent home a sense of place with one-of-a-kind quilts to keep with them wherever they go. Our goal is to provide a personal, beautiful resting spot no matter where the child is. Everyone, large and small, needs a rest after an eventful day of playing, working, learning, and making.

The projects in this chapter are just right for cozy downtime. They may possibly inspire your children to slow down, chill out, and take a nap. Or, they can help create a cozy spot for someone else.

Let your child help welcome a new baby into the family with the Bright Hopes for Baby Blanket (page 152) or make a stack to donate to your local shelter. Abscond with one of your pre-schooler's house drawings and sew a surprise There's No Place Like Home Pillow (page 134), a

soft reminder of his own home or a place in his imagination. Help an industrious teen make Twice the Smiles Quilts (page 146) for herself and a close friend or to give away to someone in need. The Reading Time Quilt (page 140) is infinitely flexible, depending on the fabrics you and your child choose. Make it again and again as a go-to gift.

When you make a quilt with your children you will have a front-row seat to their understanding. They often have a difficult time

imagining how in the world all those little pieces are going to fit together to make a huge quilt. When it begins to grow as they sew, you can see the discovery on their faces.

The world can be harsh, and nothing soothes a weary soul better than a safe, warm bed with a pillow, blanket, or quilt. Tuck your little one into bed with a quilt that you made together, and your heart will be very full indeed.

MATERIALS

* Felt and felted wool knits and wovens; quantities depend on your drawing

* ¼ yd (23 cm) of lightweight fusible interfacing

* Trim such as rickrack, ribbons, and buttons

* Embroidery floss

* Cotton or polyester fill

* Coordinating thread

* Contrasting thread

TOOLS

* Basic Sewing Kit

* Children's house drawings

* X-acto knife

* Edgestitch foot (optional)

FINISHED SIZE

Pillows vary according to your drawing. Mine range from 9" × 6" (23 × 15 cm) to 30" × 13" (76 × 33 cm).

There's No Place Like Home Pillows

Kids love to draw houses and castles and skyscrapers and tents. These drawings translate perfectly into fabulous pillows. The large basic shapes and fun details make them a great way to try drafting your own patterns. If you haven't already tried "fearless sewing," now is the time!

These pillows will be as much at home on your couch as on your child's bed. Consider a tiny house pillow as a pincushion or a super large one as a body pillow. Guide an older child through making one on his own. The variety of techniques to use makes this project almost like a sewing sampler. Kids can also simply embroider a few elements and handsew around the entire pillow.

Kid Work

★ Draw houses
★ Choose fabrics and trims
★ Sew the pillows

Your child's house drawings will be different than my child's house drawings, so these instructions are more like guidelines and suggestions. The instructions go through the construction of a pillow from one of my daughter's drawings, the turquoise, red, and green house pictured on page 134. You should adapt these techniques to use with your kids' drawings, making your pillows as small or as large as you like.

You are looking for the feel of the drawing, not necessarily an exact copy. Use your sewing knowledge to alter the drawing to fit the techniques you are using. For example, in a different Home Pillow, the house drawing was reproduced full size, but the flowers were too small to sew. So I enlarged some of the flower pictures to 200% and others to 250%. The essence remains the same.

1 Choose a drawing and either copy it full size or enlarge it to the size you would like your pillow.

2 Draw on top of your full-size pattern, outlining the basic main sections. This will help you decide which elements in the drawing to use and make clear delineations between the pieces.

This is the time to think about assembly so you will know how to

cut each piece. Larger areas, like the front of the house and the roof, can be cut out separately and butt joined (see Tools and Techniques, page 19). Smaller features, like doors or windows, can be appliquéd or inlayed into a cutout in the background piece. Because all stitching is visible, there are no seam allowances on any of the pieces.

3 Cut the pattern into the large pieces along the lines. Cut out doors and windows using an X-acto knife if the feature, such as a window, is not next to the edge. This will leave holes in your large piece that can be used later as a stencil when you are placing the elements.

4 Assemble the felt and felted wool for your specific drawing.

5 Cut the pieces from your chosen fabrics. For butt joining and inlay, cut each piece separately. With appliqué, cut the bottom piece in its entirety, as well as the piece to appliqué.

In this Home Pillow, I cut out one orange roof, one blue side, one green window, and one orange window. I left the larger orange roof and blue side pieces whole because there is no inlay in those pieces. I inlayed the small orange window into the larger green window, so I cut the orange window shape out of the green window.

To make the sewing of inlay and butt-joined pieces easier and the joints stronger, cut a strip of fusible interfacing large enough to cover the area to be sewn. Turn over the two pieces to be joined and match the cut edges. Lay the interfacing fusible side down to cover the seams and fuse.

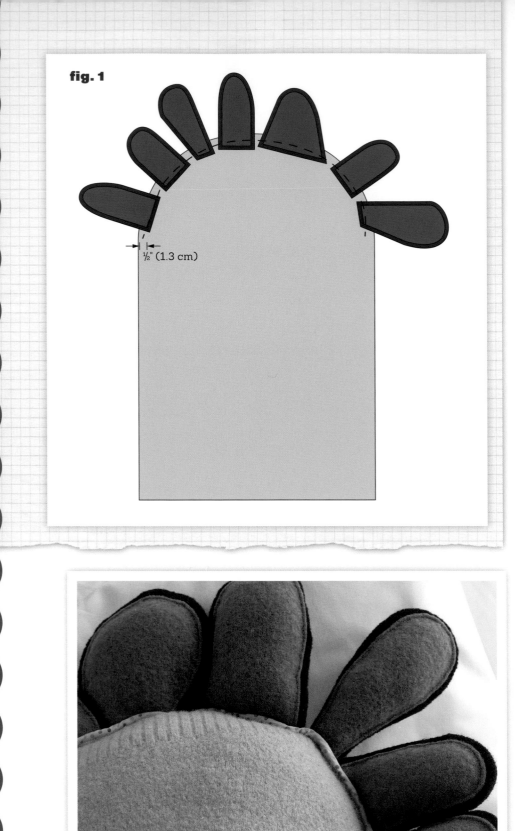

fig. 1

½" (1.3 cm)

6 Turn the pieces over and zigzag stitch the seams, right side up.

7 Appliqué any additional elements such as doors, windows, and shutters. Transfer details, such as stars or shingles on the roof, lines around the house, or a face in a window. Embroider them on the pillow top.

Be creative in adding details. You can topstitch ribbons or bias tape for bolder lines and add a button for a doorknob or whatever other architectural elements your Home Pillow needs.

8 To cut the back, use the assembled front as a pattern. You can also piece the back using the same patterns you used for the front.

9 To sew the pillow together, first baste any appendages onto the inside of the back (see the sidebar on page 139). Overlap the bottom edge of the appendage with the outer edge of the back by ½" (1.3 cm) and baste them on **(FIGURE 1)**. Then match the front and back with wrong sides together and pin. Topstitch around the pillows, leaving the bottom open for stuffing.

10 To finish, stuff the pillow and handsew the bottom closed with an overcast or blanket stitch. Alternatively, stuff the pillow and push the stuffing to the top. Pin the bottom closed and machine topstitch the opening. Shake the pillow to even out the stuffing.

Fabulous Extras

Some drawings may have things sticking out from the tops or sides of the building. Some you may recognize as chimneys or flowers, but others may just be triangles, scallops, pointy things, appendages . . . whatever. Whatever your children imagine in, on, or around their fanciful houses, you can translate into wool or felt. The architecture of your Home Pillow is not constrained by the usual rules of home building!

To make your child's imaginative appendages, simply cut the pieces separately from a single layer of wool or felt. Insert them into the pillow's seam when you sew the front and the back of the house together. The roof isn't the only place ripe for embellishment! You can also add fabulous extras into any seam or under a ribbon or appliqué.

If you want to give the chimney, wafts of smoke, or lightning bolts more weight, stuff them separately from the rest of the house. Cut two matching or coordinating layers for the appendage and topstitch around the outside, leaving the bottom open. Stuff, but leave space near the opening unstuffed so you can sew the appendage into the main body of the pillow. Insert that bottom edge into the seam when you sew the front and the back together.

To make flowers, start with the stem. Place two lengths of wide ribbon together and topstitch down both long edges. Then pull cotton cord through the ribbon tube as stuffing; a metal loop turner is helpful here.

Cut flowers from a double layer of felt, then add details such as French knots to the front of the flower. Pin the two flower pieces wrong sides together,

inserting one end of the stem in between. Topstitch around the outside of the flower.

You can make leaves, too, which can be added to your flower or used alone. Also cut the leaves from two layers of

felt, then machine stitch down their centers to create a vein. Attach the leaves and flowers to the pillow in the seams as any other appendage. Combine with appliqués and embroidery to create a whole garden!

MATERIALS

* 6 images from a cotton novelty print for block centers

* 1 yd (91.5 cm) total of coordinating fabric and scraps for crazy Log Cabin strips

* ¼ yd (23 cm) of contrasting fabric for inner border

* 1 yd (91.5 cm) total of coordinating fabric and scraps for outer border

* 1¾ yd (1.6 m) of 44" (112 cm) wide cotton fabric for backing

* ½ yd (45.5 cm) of cotton fabric for binding

* 44" × 58" (112 × 147.5 cm) piece of batting

* Coordinating thread

TOOLS

* Basic Sewing Kit

* Walking foot (optional)

FINISHED SIZE

My Reading Time Quilt is 40" × 54" (101.5 × 137 cm). Sew twelve blocks, instead of six, to make a quilt that is 54" × 68" (137 × 173 cm).

Reading Time Quilt

The e-mail came in midsummer before my daughter started kindergarten. Her new teacher sent a list of all the supplies she would need. And there it was, in between a box of crayons and a set of watercolors: a small blanket for rest and reading time. Just what I needed! I may have been sending my baby off into the big world, but at least she would have love in the form of a quilt made by me. I planned a crazy Log Cabin quilt with fussy-cut animals in the center of the blocks. The animals would be her friends to keep her company, the quilt would be full of lots of color and patterns for fun, and a hand-embroidered label would be a special touch just from me.

I planned the quilt as a surprise, but somehow she figured it out and wanted to help. My disappointment was quickly replaced by the joy we had making it together. She decided which fabric should go next, handing me strips as I sewed. The Reading Time Quilt is the perfect project to work on with kids of all ages!

Based on the traditional Log Cabin block, a crazy Log Cabin block varies widths and angles, basically setting everything askew. It is a great way to start improvisational piecing. Use a seam allowance of ¼" (6 mm), but keep in mind that this quilt is very forgiving. In fact, it's a good quilt to start a child with sewing and even rotary cutting because exact fabric sizes and seams are not vital. The exception to this is the inner border, which will need to be cut and sewn accurately.

Choose fabrics for your crazy Log Cabin centers that have animals, flowers, or other subjects your child likes. You will need six centers, so look for fabric that has six different images. Steer away from popular characters that your child will outgrow quickly. But remember, this is his or her quilt, not yours. Count out the six images you want to use and cut the fabric after that. How much fabric you need will depend on where in the print the images occur.

1 Fussy cut (see Tools and Techniques, page 24) six images from center fabric. These patches can be any size; you will add strips around until the block is the finished size. The patches can be squares, rectangles, or any kind of odd straight-sided shape. The centers shown in my Reading Time Quilt range from 4" × 7" (10 × 18 cm) to 5" × 8¼" (12.5 × 21 cm). Keep in mind that you will lose ¼" (6 mm) all around for the seam allowance, and you don't want to lose any of the image.

2 Cut the fabric for the rest of the crazy Log Cabin blocks into strips 2–4" (5–10 cm) wide. Keep the lengths long because you will trim them off as you sew.

3 Now you will sew each block. Choose a strip that is at least as long as or longer than the side of your first center piece. Place one strip onto one side, right sides together with any excess extending beyond the center piece. Sew. Press seam toward the new strip. Trim off excess that goes beyond the end.

4 Work your way around each center image, adding strips. Angle the strips as you go, skewing them to create the off-kilter crazy Log Cabin effect. If you have strips that are not long enough, you can piece them together with other strips by matching and sewing the short ends. You can also use some of the small details from the center fabric by inserting scraps of them in between other strips.

You do not need to work each side in order, but you can add extra strips on some sides to shift the center off so it's not in the exact center of the square. Stop when each block is at least 14½" (37 cm) on all sides. Even though the center can be off-kilter, the finished block must be square.

5 Trim the blocks to exactly 14½" (37 cm) square. You can also join two smaller blocks together and then add a long piece to span them both. Treat this like a double-size

fig. 1

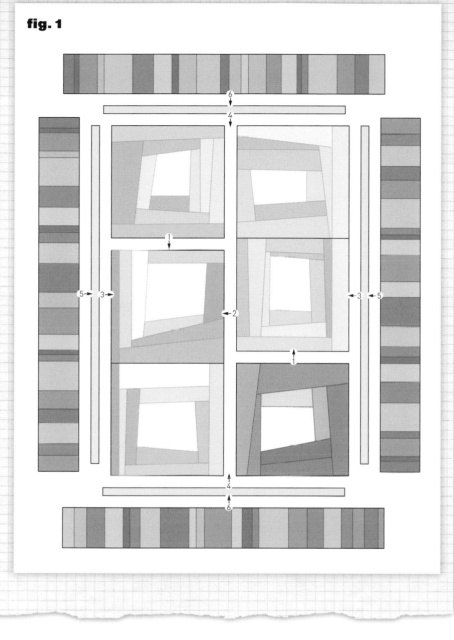

★ Choose fabrics
★ Hand strips to sewist
★ Arrange blocks
★ Sew the blocks

8 Cut the fabric for the outer border into 5½" (14 cm) lengths and a variety of widths ranging from 1" to 3" (2.5–7.5 cm). Sew the outer border strips together, joining long sides until you have one long piece. Cut that long piece into four sections: two sections that are each 44" (112 cm) long and two sections that are each 40½" (103 cm) long.

Sew the 44" (112 cm) strips onto the two long sides of the quilt top. Press seams toward the inner border. Sew the 40½" (103 cm) long borders onto the two short sides. Press seams toward inner border.

9 Pin the top of the quilt to the batting and the backing (see Tools and Techniques, page 22), and then quilt as desired. For my Reading Time Quilt, I valley stitched (my name for stitching in the ditch) around the block centers and on both sides of the inner border. Then I free-motion quilted cloud shapes in the blocks and the outer border. The fabric my daughter and I chose for the binding has rows of flowers, so I cut the binding carefully along the rows to have the flowers create a frame around the quilt.

Don't forget to add a special name tag on the back!

block and trim to 14½" × 28½" (37 × 72.5 cm). I did that in my quilt with the elephant and the lion block and the hippo and the giraffe block.

6 Arrange the blocks as desired. Sew blocks vertically into two rows of three 14" (35.5 cm) blocks and then sew the rows together **(FIGURE 1)**. Press.

7 Cut two inner border strips 1½" × 42½" (3.8 × 108 cm) and two inner border strips 1½" × 30½" (3.8 × 77.5 cm).

Sew the longer inner border strips onto the two long sides of the quilt top. Press the seams toward the border. Sew the shorter inner border strips onto the two short sides, and press the seams toward the border.

The Eighteen-Year Quilt

Do you make beautiful photo albums and scrapbooks or write loving journal entries to your children every night? Well, I don't. I try, really. I want to be one of those parents. When our older daughter was born, I tried the journal thing. It lasted about three days. I remembered our pile of wedding photos that has been sitting in the same bag since 1995 and decided to accept reality. I am a maker, I reminded myself. I need to make her something to mark her childhood. I'll make her a special quilt.

I have always been a fan of hand appliqué, but never took the time to perfect the technique. But I can surely manage to make one hand-appliquéd block each year. When my daughter turns eighteen, I will have an entire handsewn quilt top to give her. Then I will have the four years she is in college to quilt it! And so I began the Eighteen-Year Quilt.

Each block is an 18" (45.5 cm) square oriented on point. Because we like to garden, I planned the quilt around the growing season where we live. Each block will be a different flower, starting with the earliest blooming flowers and ending with the last flower at the end of the season. I started with crocus and am working

through daffodils, tulips, and my grandmother's Blaze roses.

Every year, I go into the garden with my notebook and pencil at the time of year just following the previous year's block. I wander the garden looking for what my daughter is especially fond of at the time. I make a quick sketch and then search for fabric.

Actually appliquéing the block usually takes me until the following year. I have been known to work on several at once, but it does get done eventually. Each year when I lay out the completed blocks, my daughter and I can see her quilt grow, creating an entire garden.

Because I already had a plan, when my second daughter was born I started sewing her first block when I was still in the hospital. She is getting flowers also, but different ones, and the blocks are set straight on in different sizes: hellebores, chionodoxa, and a straight-on view of the center of the tulip she put her face into the year she turned three.

Plan your own Eighteen-Year Quilt based on what is meaningful to you and your family. Look to animals, constellations, or symbols for your inspiration. If your children are older, make a Ten-Year Quilt, a Five-Year Quilt, or a One-Year Quilt instead. Make one block for each special occasion you celebrate throughout the year. Don't want to appliqué? Use embroidery, patchwork, or even fabric markers on a solid ground. Use what works for you!

As your quilt grows, you will see how your sewing skills have improved over the course of the quilt and how your design sensibilities change. Your quilt will be a record of you and your work, reflecting your child growing up, a reminder of his favorites and the early years. It's an amazing gift for a child you love!

MATERIALS

* 4 yd (3.7 m) of fabric A for Quilt 1 and Quilt 2

* 4 yd (3.7 m) of fabric B for Quilt 1 and Quilt 2

* 1 yd (91.5 cm) of fabric C for Quilt 1 and Quilt 2

* ¾ yd (68.5 cm) of binding fabric for Quilt 1

* ¾ yd (68.5 cm) of binding fabric for Quilt 2

* 68" × 84" (173 × 213 cm) piece of batting for Quilt 1

* 68" × 84" (173 × 213 cm) piece of batting for Quilt 2

* 4 yd (3.7 m) of backing fabric for Quilt 1

* 4 yd (3.7 m) of backing fabric for Quilt 2

* Coordinating thread

TOOLS

* Basic Sewing Kit

* Walking foot

* Cut-resistant glove

FINISHED SIZE

Each quilt is 63" × 79" (160 × 201 cm).

Twice the Smiles Quilts

One of the best parts about making wonderful things is giving them away. With this project, you can cut and sew two quilts at the same time, creating two different but coordinating quilts. Choose two main fabrics and one accent fabric. The two main fabrics switch places with each other as you construct the quilts, but the accent fabric is in the same place in both quilts. One quilt is basically the negative of the other. Use different backing and binding fabrics for each quilt to make them unique, or use the same fabric for both quilts to make a matched set.

This is the perfect project for a teenager to make with just a little guidance from you. The instructions give specific cutting and sewing steps to make it easier for your child to be independent. She gets to keep one quilt and then give the other away to a sibling or a friend or donate it to a child in need. Twice the smiles!

I love to use rich, bold solids and save the crazy prints as a surprise for the backing and binding. Here, solid-shot cotton provides depth of color. But no matter what color palette you prefer, these quilts are adaptable to all kinds of color combinations, including softer tones and lots of white. You can, of course, use tone-on-tone fabrics or even prints for the quilt top.

The fabric amounts and instructions for cutting fabrics A, B, and C will yield enough squares and rectangles for two quilts. Fabric amounts for the backing and binding are for each quilt in case you want to use different fabrics. If you want to use the same fabrics to back and bind both quilts, just double the amounts.

1 Fold fabric A in half lengthwise, matching the selvedge edges. Fold it lengthwise again. You now have four layers of fabric. Starting at one short end of the folded fabric, square up the end: line up the long bottom folded edge of the fabric with the edge of a gridded ruler, then cut up the perpendicular edge of the

ruler to trim off a small strip of the folded fabric from the short edge.

2 Keep the fabric folded and cut seven strips 9½" (24 cm) wide, cutting through all four layers. If your rotary blade is sharp, it should cut through the four layers easily; change to a new blade if necessary. Use a cut-resistant glove on your hand holding the ruler for safety and extra traction.

Turn the first folded strip 90 degrees and cut off the folds and selvedge edges from one side. Then measure 9½" (24 cm) from that side and cut to make four 9½" (24 cm) squares. Repeat with the remaining strips until you have twenty-eight squares. You will have fabric left over to use in the next two steps.

3 Also from fabric A, cut seven 6½" (16.5 cm) wide strips, keeping the fabric folded and cutting through all four layers. Turn the first folded strip 90 degrees and cut off the folds and selvedge edges from one side. Measure 9½" (24 cm) and cut to make four 6½" × 9½" (16.5 ×

24 cm) rectangles. Repeat with the remaining strips until you have twenty-eight rectangles.

4 Cut seven more strips from fabric A, this time 3½" (9 cm) wide, keeping the fabric folded and cutting through all four layers. Turn the first folded strip 90 degrees and cut off the folds and selvedge edges from one side. Measure 9½" (24 cm) and cut to make four 3½" × 9½" (9 × 24 cm) rectangles. Repeat with the remaining strips until you have twenty-eight rectangles.

5 Repeat all of the previous steps using fabric B.

fig. 1

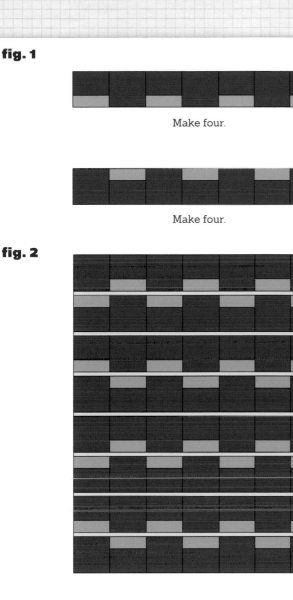

Make four.

Make four.

fig. 2

Assemble the Quilt Tops

9 Now you are ready to assemble the quilt tops. For Quilt 1, sew each 3½" (9 cm) strip to one 6½" (16.5 cm) strip, matching the 9½" (24 cm) sides. The blocks are now 9½" (24 cm) square. Press the blocks.

10 Do the same with the strips in your Quilt 2 pile.

11 For each quilt, alternate the pieced blocks with the 9½" (24 cm) squares to make eight rows of seven blocks each **(FIGURE 1)**. Four of the rows will have four pieced blocks and three 9½" (24 cm) squares, and four of the rows will have three pieced blocks and four 9½" (24 cm) squares.

Sew the rows together, adding a strip of fabric C between the pieced rows **(FIGURE 2)**. Press the seams toward fabric C.

12 Now you are ready to finish the quilts. See Tools and Techniques (page 22) for instructions on pinning a quilt top, batting, and backing together, and for finishing techniques.

These quilts can be machine-quilted, like mine, hand-quilted, or tied. The graphic design of the quilts lends itself to simple lines and geometric patterns for the quilting, which makes a great introduction to machine quilting. My quilts have simple lines spaced just 1" (2.5 cm) apart. One quilt has vertical lines and the other has horizontal lines.

Use a walking foot with a stitch guide to keep the lines evenly spaced or just eyeball it for some extra wonki-ness. Be sure to take advantage of the binding for extra fun with color and pattern.

6 Make a fabric A pile and a fabric B pile. Swap the 3½" × 9½" (9 × 24 cm) strips in each pile. The stacks will now be called Quilt 1 and Quilt 2.

7 Fold fabric C in half lengthwise, matching the selvedge edges. Fold lengthwise again. Starting at one short end of the folded fabric, square up the end as in Step 1.

8 Cut twenty-one strips 1½" (3.8 cm) wide. Cut seven of these fabric C strips in half width-wise to make fourteen strips. Match each of the fourteen remaining long strips with one of the fourteen short strips. Sew together on the short ends to make fourteen extra-long strips. Trim each of these to 63½" (161.5 cm) long. Put seven strips onto the Quilt 1 pile and seven onto the Quilt 2 pile.

Pillowcases Three Ways

A matching pillowcase is a quick and simple way to make the gift of a quilt extra special. You can highlight a favorite fabric from the quilt or introduce a different yet coordinating bold print. I am not a fan of using trendy novelty prints for quilts because children outgrow them so quickly. Instead, I like to use them for a pillowcase for minimal commitment. Kids can even make this simple project themselves. In a bit of time after school, they can make brand-new pillowcases all by themselves by bedtime. A pillowcase is a great gift even without the quilt. Bring on the bedtime smiles with a surprise pillowcase and new book on your child's bed!

MATERIALS
* 1–2 yd (91.5 cm–1.8 m) of cotton fabric

* Coordinating thread

TOOLS
* Basic Sewing Kit

FINISHED SIZE
These pillowcases are about 21" × 32" (53.5 × 81.5 cm), depending on the exact width of your fabric. They will fit most standard pillows.

Icing on the Cake Pillowcase

This simple, modern pillowcase is just right with your Twice the Smiles quilt. You'll need 1 yd (91.5 cm) of fabric for the body and ¼ yd (23 cm) for the border along the top edge. Use a ½" (1.3 cm) seam allowance.

① Fold 1 yd (91.5 cm) of fabric in half lengthwise with right sides together and selvedges matching. Trim both ends to square up the fabric. With the fabric still folded, measure its length. Trim off about 4½" (11.5 cm) from the selvedge edges, keeping the fabric square. Unfold the fabric. For the contrasting border, cut one strip 8½" (21.5 cm) wide by the length of the fabric you just measured.

② With right sides together, pin one long edge of the border-fabric strip to one long edge of the main fabric. Pin the remaining long edge of the border fabric to the remaining long edge of the main fabric and sew. You now have a big tube.

③ With right sides together, match the two long seams so the main fabric is folded in half lengthwise and the border fabric is folded in half lengthwise. Sew one of the short ends closed.

④ On the remaining open side, fold up the hem ½" (1.3 cm) and then again 3½" (9 cm) to make a wide hem. Topstitch around the hem, then turn the pillowcase right side out and press.

Super Simple Pillowcase

This is the easy-peasy, fifteen-minute, was-that-all? pillowcase. You can make it with a single piece of 1 yd (91.5 cm) of fabric.

① Fold 1 yd (91.5 cm) of fabric in half lengthwise with right sides together and selvedges matching. Trim both ends to square up the fabric. Sew down one short end of the folded fabric and then down the selvedge

side of the folded fabric, using a ½" (1.3 cm) seam allowance.

② On the remaining open side, fold up the hem ½" (1.3 cm) and then again 3½" (9 cm) to make a wide hem. Last, topstitch around the hem. Turn the pillowcase right side out and press. Do a happy dance.

Rickrack Block Pillowcase

A few extra minutes and some jumbo rickrack make this pillowcase extra fun. You need ¾ yd (68.5 cm) of fabric for the main block, ½ yd (45.5 cm) of fabric for the border block, and 1¼ yd (1.1 m) of jumbo rickrack. Use a ½" (1.3 cm) seam allowance.

① Fold the main block fabric in half lengthwise with right sides together and selvedges matching. Trim one cut end to square up the fabric. Then, measure 22½" (57 cm) from the trimmed end and cut all the way across.

② Square up one cut edge of the border block fabric. Then cut one strip 11½" (29 cm) wide and one strip 4½" (11.5 cm) wide, both from selvedge to selvedge, from the border block fabric. You are cutting the border and the border lining from the border block fabric.

③ Lay out the 11½" (29 cm) strip with right side up and then place the rickrack on one of the long edges. Keep the rickrack 1" (2.5 cm) from each end, tucking the cut ends into the seam allowance. Lay the 4½" (11.5 cm) strip right side down on top of the rickrack to sandwich it in between the two fabrics. Sew down the length of the sandwich using a ½" (1.3 cm) seam allowance. Open the fabric and carefully press the rickrack toward the 4½" (11.5 cm) strip and the seam allowance toward the 11½" (29 cm) strip.

④ Match the free cut edge of the 11½" (29 cm) border strip with a cut edge of the 22½" (57 cm) main fabric, right sides together. If one of the fabrics is wider than the other from selvedge to selvedge, trim the wider fabric even with the narrower fabric. Press the seam toward the main block fabric. If desired, topstitch this seam. You now have one large piece with main fabric, border, and border lining all sewn together.

⑤ Fold the pieced fabric in half lengthwise with right sides together and selvedges matching. Sew down the free short end of the folded main block fabric. Then stitch down the long selvedge side of the main block fabric and the two sections of border block.

⑥ On the remaining open side, fold up the hem first ½" (1.3 cm) and then again 3½" (9 cm) to make a wide hem. The rickrack makes a lovely trim along the edge. Adjust the width of the hem if necessary so the rickrack is right on the edge. Finally, topstitch around the hem. Turn the pillowcase and press.

MATERIALS

* 1 yd (91.5 cm) of plush or fleece fabric for top

* 1 yd (91.5 cm) of flannel for backing

* ¼ yd (23 cm) of satin for edging

* Scraps of ¼–1" (6 mm–2.5 cm) wide ribbon for edging

* Fabric scraps for prairie point edging

* Coordinating thread

TOOLS

* Basic Sewing Kit

* Walking foot

FINISHED SIZE

This blanket is 29" × 35" (73.5 × 89 cm), not including the prairie point and ribbon loop edging.

Bright Hopes for Baby Blanket

The Bright Hopes Collaborative Quilt Project is an organization my mother, Eileen Fisher, and I started to make one-of-a-kind quilts for foster children and homeless families living in temporary housing. We now have many volunteers who sew Bright Hopes Quilts as well as Bright Hopes for Baby Blankets.

I designed the soft and tuckable Bright Hopes for Baby Blankets for newborn babies. The blankets are plush on one side and flannel on the other. They are sure to remain a favorite even as the baby grows. Your child can help you make a few assembly-line style—one for a new sibling, one for a gift, and a few to donate to your local shelter.

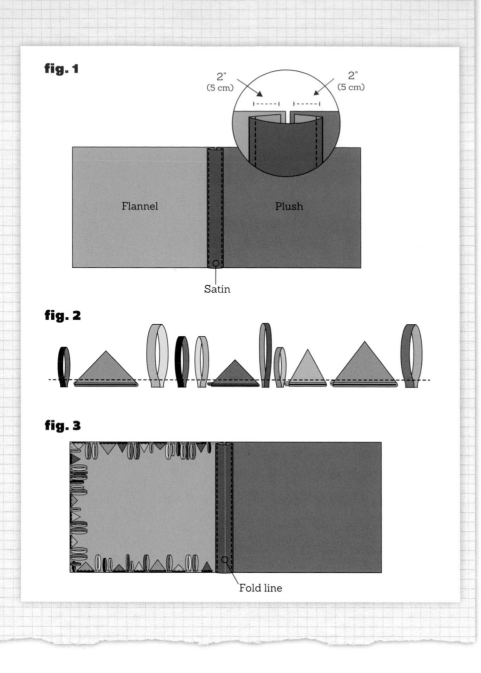

fig. 1

2"
(5 cm)

2"
(5 cm)

Flannel

Plush

Satin

fig. 2

fig. 3

Fold line

flannel and one piece of plush each 30" × 36" (76 × 91.5 cm).

2 On the wrong side of the satin, draw a pencil line lengthwise 2" (5 cm) from each long edge. You will have 4" (10 cm) between the lines. This will be your seam allowance.

3 Pin one long edge of the satin to one short side of the flannel, right sides together. Pin in the 2" (5 cm) seam allowance directly on the pencil line, but not past the pencil line to avoid making holes in the satin. Sew just on the pencil line.

Repeat for the other long edge of satin, sewing it to a short side of the plush with right sides together.

4 Topstitch the satin on both long edges, catching the plush and flannel underneath on each side **(FIGURE 1)**.

Make the Prairie Point and Ribbon Edging

5 Cut twenty-five fabric scraps into squares of sizes varying from about 2" (5 cm) square to 4" (10 cm) square. Fold the squares into triangles with wrong sides together and then into triangles again so all the raw edges are on one side. Press the triangles.

6 Cut ribbon into twenty-five pieces in a variety of lengths from 2" to 3" (5–7.5 cm). Fold the ribbon pieces in half widthwise, matching the raw edges.

7 Using a ¼" (6 mm) seam allowance, sew the triangles and ribbons into a long string, feeding the triangles and ribbons into the sewing machine as you stitch. Feed the triangles and ribbons in randomly,

Plush fabric like Minky is usually sold in 60" (152.5 cm) widths, so you can get two blankets from 1 yd (91.5 cm) of fabric. If you only want to make one blanket, some retailers sell blanket-size pieces of Minky already cut to 30" × 36" (76 × 91.5 cm).

Be sure not to iron the plush. Keep it fluffy! Due to the shifty nature of

plush and satin, this project requires lots of pins. You may need to pin every inch or so. Make sure you remove all of the pins when you are done. Feel free to baste instead if you prefer. Using a walking foot for sewing is especially helpful with such slippery fabrics.

1 Cut one piece of satin 30" × 8" (76 × 20.5 cm). Cut one piece of

making sure to catch all raw edges in the seam **(FIGURE 2)**.

Cut the triangle and ribbon string into three pieces. Two pieces should each be 34" (86.5 cm) long or less. The third piece should be 29" (73.5 cm) long or less.

Assemble the Blanket

8 Pin the triangle and ribbon strings to the right side of the flannel so the raw edges of the triangles and ribbons match the raw edges of the flannel. The triangles and ribbons should point inward. Match the 29" (73.5 cm) piece to the bottom short side of the flannel. Align the 34" (86.5 cm) pieces with the two long sides of the flannel. Baste the triangles and ribbons to the flannel using a ¼" (6 mm) seam allowance **(FIGURE 3)**.

9 Fold the entire blanket in half down the middle of the length of the satin with right sides together. Match the three edges of the plush and the flannel. Pin.

10 Using a ½" (1.3 cm) seam allowance, sew from one top corner down the side, turn the corner, and sew just 12" (30.5 cm) along the bottom of the blanket. Do the same on the other side. This will leave an opening on the bottom. Clip the four corners carefully.

Finish the Blanket

11 Turn the blanket right sides out and carefully push out the corners. Fold in the raw edges of the opening and handsew the opening closed.

12 With the plush on the bottom and the flannel on the top, finish the blanket with

topstitching. Using thread that matches the flannel, topstitch the blanket ½" (1.3 cm) from the edge on the three sides with the plush and flannel, but not on the satin.

Kid Work

★ Select fabrics and ribbons
★ Fold and sew prairie points and ribbons

Resources

Searching for materials in person is really the best way to determine a fabric's true color, a pattern's scale, and the overall quality of the material. You may be surprised by how much great stuff you can find in your local thrift, hardware, craft, and fabric stores as well as in your own stash. Sometimes, of course, you must go beyond your local resources to find just the perfect materials. These online resources may be helpful.

Fabrics and Trims

G Street Fabrics
gstreetfabrics.com

Glorious Color
gloriouscolor.com

Jo-Ann Fabric and Craft Stores
joann.com

M & J Trimming
mjtrim.com

Mary Jo's Cloth Store
maryjos.com

The Minky Boutique
theminkyboutique.com

Mood Designer Fabrics
moodfabrics.com

Purl Soho
purlsoho.com

Super Buzzy
superbuzzy.com

Tinsel Trading Company
tinseltrading.com

Batting and Fill

Quiltbug Quilt Shop
quiltbug.com

Fabric Markers and Paints

Dharma Trading
dharmatrading.com

Wool Roving and Felt Balls

Weir Dolls & Crafts
weirdollsandcrafts.com

Cut-Resistant Gloves

Fons and Porter's Quilt Supply
shopfonsandporter.com

Printable Graph Paper

Incompetech
incompetech.com

Children's Books to Inspire Your Family

I have long embraced the mixed-media approach to living and learning as well as making. Children's books have always been a favorite of mine, even before I had my own kids. Reinforce the love of making things your own way and being your own you by reading wonderful children's books with your kids. Here are a few of my family's favorites.

The Big Orange Splot
written and illustrated by
Daniel Manus Pinkwater
New York: Scholastic, 1977.

Extra Yarn
written by Mac Barnett and
illustrated by Jon Klassen
New York: HarperCollins, 2012.

A Day with No Crayons
written by Elizabeth Rusch and
illustrated by Chad Cameron
Lanham, MD: Rising Moon, 2007.

Odd Velvet
written by Mary Whitcomb and
illustrated by Tara Calahan King
San Francisco: Chronicle Books, 2007.

The Cloud Spinner
written by Michael Catchpool and
illustrated by Alison Jay
New York: Knopf, 2012.

The Quiltmaker's Gift and
The Quiltmaker's Journey
written by Jeff Brumbeau and
illustrated by Gail de Marcken
New York: Scholastic, 2001 and 2004.

Woolbur
written by Leslie Helakoski and
illustrated by Lee Harper
New York: HarperCollins, 2008.

Knitting Nell
written and illustrated by
Julie Jersild Roth
New York: Houghton Mifflin, 2006.

Charlie Needs a Cloak
written and illustrated by
Tomie dePaola
New York: Houghton Mifflin, 2006.

Fanny and *Fanny & Annabelle*
written and illustrated by Holly Hobbie
New York: Little, Brown, 2008 and
2009.

The Keeping Quilt
written and illustrated by
Patricia Polacco
New York: Simon & Schuster, 2001.

Deborah Fisher
and Her Nonprofit Organizations

Deborah Fisher grew up sewing dolls, making odd things, and watching her mother make quilts. She has a BFA from the Maryland Institute College of Art and an MFA from Cranbrook Academy of Art. After fifteen years working as a fine artist, she now designs the dolls and odd things she's always loved to make as well as quilts.

Deborah also leads two nonprofit organizations that provide hand made quilts and dolls to underprivileged children. She is the director and quilt designer for the Bright Hopes Collaborate Quilt Project, which she co-founded with her mother Eileen Fisher in 2003, and she launched Bo Twal in 2013 to bring handmade dolls to children internationally.

Maybe a quilt could give people who have no permanent home at all a piece of home, a sense of place, to carry with them wherever they go. So, she asked her mother if she wanted to make quilts together to donate. She had never made a quilt, but she stumbled around, got a rotary cutter, and started designing one-of-a-kind quilt kits to be sewn by friends who volunteered to join them. Since then, Deborah has designed more than 500 quilts for Bright Hopes.

The **Bright Hopes Collaborative Quilt Project** now has three community-based programs.

Through QuiltGIVING, they make one-of-a-kind quilts that are given to homeless children living in temporary shelters. The quilts are theirs to keep wherever they go. Bright Hopes for Baby blankets for newborns are also donated through QuiltGIVING.

With QuiltCOMMUNITY, Bright Hopes partners with other groups such as scouts and differently-abled adults in day treatment programs to teach sewing and to make quilts to donate through QuiltGIVING. They also work with students on community service projects.

QuiltWORKS offers on-site quilting workshops for individuals living in shelters or other temporary housing. With QuiltWORKS, each participant makes his or her own quilt to keep.

You can find out more about the Bright Hopes Collaborative Quilt Project at brighthopes.org.

Bright Hopes Collaborative Quilt Project

In 2002, Deborah was at a three-month artist residency in Wisconsin and had brought a quilt that her husband's aunt had made. She was living in a strange house, with other artists she didn't know. Putting that quilt on her bed made it feel like home.

These handmade blankets were donated to homeless newborns through QuiltGIVING. You can make your own baby blanket with the project on page 152.

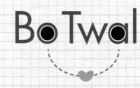

Bo Twal

Bo Twal grew from Deborah's long-term love of sewing dolls and interest in giving more internationally. *Bo Twal*, which means "cloth kiss" in Haitian Creole, provides handmade